Polymer
Pizzazz 2

25
Beautiful jewelry projects to make and wear

KB

KALMBACH BOOKS

Kalmbach Books
21027 Crossroads Circle
Waukesha, Wisconsin 53186
www.Kalmbach.com/Books

Published in 2011
15 14 13 12 11   1 2 3 4 5

Manufactured in the United States of America

ISBN: 978-0-87116-426-1

The material in this book has appeared previously in *Bead&Button* and *Art Jewelry* magazines. *Bead&Button* and *Art Jewelry* are registered as a trademark.

Please follow appropriate health and safety measures. Some general guidelines are presented in this book, but always read and follow manufacturers' instructions. Every effort has been made to ensure the accuracy of the information presented; however, the publisher is not responsible for any injuries, losses, or other damages that may result from the use of the information in this book.

Publisher's Cataloging-in-Publication Data

Polymer pizzazz. 2, 25 beautiful jewelry projects to make and wear / [compiled by Kalmbach Books].

   p. : col. ill. ; cm.

The material in this book has appeared previously in Bead&Button and Art Jewelry magazines.
ISBN: 978-0-87116-426-1

   1. Polymer clay craft–Handbooks, manuals, etc. 2. Jewelry making. I. Kalmbach Publishing Company. II. Title: 25 beautiful jewelry projects to make and wear III. Title: Twenty-five beautiful jewelry projects to make and wear IV. Title: Bead&Button magazine. V. Title: Art Jewelry magazine.

TT297 .P26 2011
745.594/2

Contents

Introduction

Colorful, flexible, and affordable, polymer clay offers a wealth of possibilities for any jewelry artist no matter your skill level. This affordable medium is perfect for dabbling, sculpting, and shaping gorgeous jewelry. If you're new to the medium, begin with the Polymer Clay and Tools and Techniques sections; you'll learn how to condition polymer clay, make a cane, and create a Skinner blend. Refer to this section to refine your jewelry-making skills as well. You'll also find helpful tips for easy construction sprinkled throughout the projects themselves.

With 25 beautiful projects, you'll find lots of inspiration. The projects in this book are grouped by technique: Stamping & Texturing, Shaping, Caning, and Mixed Techniques. You can even expand your claymaking skills by adding metal clay. Each section offers plenty of colorful pendants, earrings, cuffs, pins, and bracelets. Whether you want a bold statement piece, like the "Extra chunky cuff," p. 14, or a whimsical focal, like the "June bug pin," p. 70, you're sure to see the perfect jewelry to fit your taste.

Polymer clay

About polymer clay

Polymer clay is a synthetic, modeling compound made of polyvinyl chloride (PVC), pigments, and a plasticizer. The plasticizer keeps the clay pliable at room temperature. When heated, the molecular structure of the PVC stabilizes, and the clay hardens. It's easy to harden the clay in a small home oven.

Polymer products

Polymer clays differ a bit from brand to brand. In general, these differences fall into the categories of firmness, flexibility, strength, color, and opacity. When selecting polymer clay, choose a product that has the properties that most complement the requirements of your specific project. You may even experiment with combining two or more brands to achieve a custom result (bake at the lowest temperature given for the brands).

Liquid polymer clay, such as translucent Liquid Sculpey or Kato Liquid Polyclay, serves as an adhesive to bond raw clay to cured clay. It is an excellent agent for transferring images, or it can be tinted and applied as a glaze before curing.

To set your work, use glazes made for polymer or a product you might have in your cabinet, such as acrylic floor finish.

A softener, such as Sculpey Diluent, Kato Clear Medium, or Fimo Mix-Quick is blended with clay to help soften it during conditioning. It also acts as a bonding agent for uncured clay.

Although polymer clay is safe to use and nontoxic, it's good practice to dedicate any tools, utensils, supplies, or appliances to the clay only. Don't use them for food.

PRODUCT	MANUFACTURER	FEATURES	WEAKNESSES	BEST USES
Fimo	Eberhard Faber	Fimo is the first polymer clay to be marketed.	Can be challenging to condition.	Fimo is a durable clay that lends itself to many projects.
Fimo Classic	Eberhard Faber	Very firm.		Excellent choice for making canes.
Fimo Soft	Eberhard Faber	Easy to condition. Some colors have glitter blended in.	Not as durable or strong as Fimo.	
Sculpey	Polyform Products	Receives paint well.	Sculpey is softer and less durable than other formulations.	
Sculpey III	Polyform Products	Soft and easy to condition; appealing matte finish.	Too soft for caning; brittle after baking	
Sculpey Super Flex	Polyform Products	Very soft and remains flexible after baking.	A bit sticky when uncured.	Flexibility after baking makes it a good candidate for mold-making.
Premo Sculpey	Polyform Products	A sophisticated range of colors and pearl metallics. Easy to condition; remains strong and relatively flexible after curing.		Great choice for a variety of techniques
Super Sculpey	Polyform Products	Hard and strong clay.		Good for sculpting.
Cernit	T&F Kunststoffe	Very hard and porcelain-like when cured; wide variety of flesh tones.	Elasticity makes it better for modeling than cane-making.	Formulated for doll makers.
Kato Polyclay	Van Aken International	Good general purpose product. Very firm and strong.		Good for making canes; rich color-mixing potential.

Tools and techniques

Use a pasta machine [a] to condition the clay and to roll pieces of clay into specific thicknesses. Settings on pasta machines vary. For example, Atlas machines have between seven and nine settings, with #1 being the thickest and #9 the thinnest. Amaco settings are the exact opposite—#1 is the thinnest and #7 is the thickest. It's a good idea to check the settings of your pasta machine so you have an approximate idea of the thickness you'll achieve with each setting. Projects use these references: thinnest, thin, medium-thin, medium, medium-thick, thick, and thickest.

Choose a smooth, durable nonstick work surface such as marble, a sheet of glass, or a smooth ceramic tile. To prevent clay from adhering to the work surface, experiment with working on parchment paper or freezer paper.

Use an acrylic roller [b] to flatten the clay. A brayer is a roller with a handle for added leverage or pressure.

Use a burnishing tool, a bone folder [c], or even the back side of a spoon to transfer an image from a transfer medium to polymer clay. Burnishing tools also will smooth and shine the clay.

Cut polymer clay with a variety of knives. A craft knife, such as an X-acto knife [d], is handy for trimming clay, creating a beveled edge, or tracing a pattern. A tissue blade [e] is an extremely sharp, smooth, and flexible blade used

SAFETY TIP: When working with a cutting blade, put painter's tape on the grip edge so you don't grab the cutting edge by mistake.

for slicing canes and cutting thin, precise layers.

After clay is rolled and ready for use, a variety of cutters help make uniform shapes and sizes. Kemper Kutters create precise, graduated sizes, and regular cookie cutters are equally useful.

Molds texture the clay and create a raised, or relief, image. Soap molds are ideal for this purpose. Additionally, you can use scrap polymer clay or a mold-maker compound to make a mold from any found object. Use a dry release, such as talc or cornstarch, on the mold so the clay casting will not stick. A spritz of water also works.

Experiment with common items to texture your clay. Carving and modeling tools, dental tools, or even a sewing machine screwdriver make unique marks in the clay. Scratch and texture sheets [f], a kitchen scouring pad, a piece of screen

[g], or rubber stamps [h] also are useful for texturing. Sculpting tools [i] help with three-dimensional modeling.

In addition to texture, you may want to add color or patina to your clay. Craft supplies such as ink pads, paints and other pigments [j], Prismacolor pencils, and decorating chalks [k] will help you enhance your design. Gold foil [l] adds elegance. A varnish or sealant protects your image.

Use a needle tool or awl to make a stringing hole in a pendant or bead. Or, punch a hole with a drinking straw. Drilling a hole in cured clay also is an option. Use a drill such as a Dremel, a spiral push drill, or a flex shaft.

Bake ("cure") polymer clay in a toaster oven or convection oven set at a low temperature to set and harden. This will be anywhere from 215–300° F; the clay packaging will have specific instructions. Confirm and monitor the accuracy of the oven's temperature with a stand-alone oven thermometer. Bake clay on a smooth surface such as cardstock or unlined index cards.

Once cured, the finished piece may need a pin-back or other embellishment, or it may become part of a larger project. Cyanoacrylate glue (superglue) provides a superior bond. Its gel form is easy to control. Other brands designed for polymer clay use include Zap-A-Gap and Sobo.

Carve cured clay with shaping tools such as those designed for cutting linoleum.

While a clay piece can be used as soon as it cools from baking, glossy polishing provides a high-quality finish. Using an electric buffing machine fitted with an unstitched muslin buff is the easiest way to get the most professional results. If you don't have access to a buffing wheel, use wet/dry sandpaper or a sanding sponge, beginning with 600 grit and progressing to finer grits. Sand your piece under water. (Very fine-grit sandpaper can be purchased at auto supply stores.) Hand polish with a sturdy fabric such as denim or polar fleece. Be sure to wear a mask when buffing, so you don't inhale any clay dust or particles.

THE RIGHT CURE

In order to get safe, successful results, bake polymer clay according to the manufacturer's specifications for the recommended temperature and time. Setting the temperature too high or baking the clay for too long can scorch the clay and release unhealthy fumes. On the other hand, if you bake your clay for too short a time or at too low a temperature, you may get an undercured piece that's weak and brittle.

Create beautiful jewelry with your polymer clay components using basic stringing and beading techniques. You'll use jewelry tools, such as crimping pliers [m]; wire cutters [n]; roundnose pliers [o] and chainnose pliers [p]. A ball peen hammer [q] and small steel bench block [r] will help you finish jewelry that uses wire.

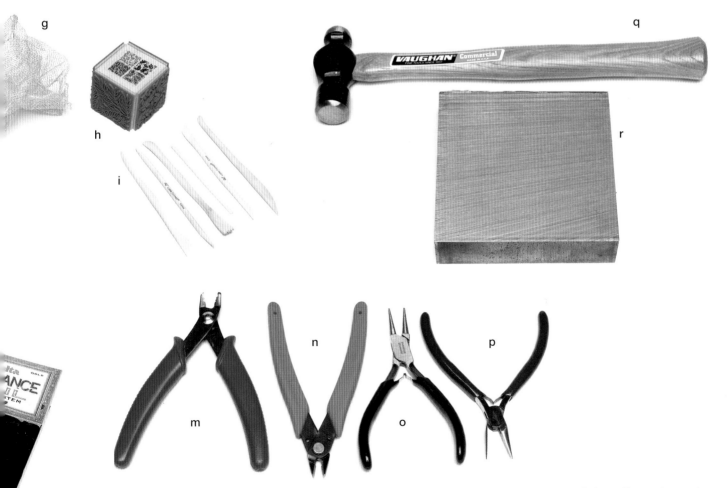

Condition polymer clay

Conditioning polymer clay softens it and makes it easier to work with. All brands of polymer clay need some conditioning before you work with them, though the degree varies among brands and depends on whether the clay is from a newly opened package or left over from another project.

You can condition clay by hand or with a pasta machine. To work it by hand, roll the clay into a ball, flatten it, then roll it into a snake. Fold the snake in half and roll it into a ball again. Continue making balls, snakes, and balls again until the clay is soft, pliable, and doesn't crack when folded.

If you use a pasta machine, most clay can be processed straight from the package. Adjust the machine to its thickest setting, then flatten one end of the clay and roll it through the machine. If the clay breaks into small pieces, press the pieces together and run them through the machine again. A long sheet of clay will form. Fold it in half and put it through the machine, fold side first, so air will not become trapped between the pieces. If air pockets form, puncture them with a needle tool and run the clay through the machine again. Twenty or more passes may be necessary to condition the clay fully, but it's easier than kneading by hand.

To make conditioning even easier, try warming the clay to make it softer. Some artists place the unopened package in their pocket or on a heating pad set to low heat. Or, use a clay-dedicated food processor to chop the clay into small pieces. Many polymer clay companies offer products that help soften the clay.

Once conditioned, roll out your desired thickness of clay using a pasta machine.

Make a cane

Canes are formed by combining different colors and shapes of clay and rolling them into a cylinder. Cut a cane in halves or fourths and layer the sections together for a more complex pattern. Reduce the cane by hand-rolling and lengthening the cylinder. Canes can begin with a diameter equal to a soda can, and then can be reduced to a diameter of an inch or smaller.

Avoid waste when you build a cane by keeping the ends trimmed throughout the process. You'll still lose five to twenty percent from the ends because they do not display the pattern as well as the middle.

Polymer clay is temperature sensitive. After you've finished making a cane, the clay will be warm. Let the cane cool before slicing, either by resting it on your workspace or by placing it in the freezer for about 90 seconds.

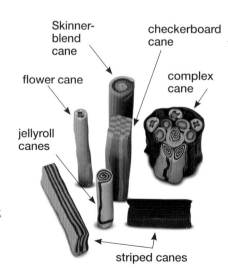

Skinner-blend cane

checkerboard cane

flower cane

complex cane

jellyroll canes

striped canes

Make a Skinner blend

Renowned polymer clay artist Judith Skinner originated this method for making clay sheets with seamless color gradations.

1 Roll equal portions of two colors separately through the thickest setting of the pasta machine. The sheets will be roughly square or rectangular.

2 Fold the sheets in half diagonally (corner to corner).

3 Stack the sheets on top of one another, lining up the folded edges. Trim the rough edges so that the two sheets become right-angle triangles.

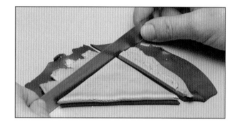

4 Separate the triangles and abut the diagonal (folded edge) sides with one another to form a square or rectangle. In order to create a sheet with unblended values of both colors, offset the placement slightly so that the corners do not meet. Trim the corners.

5 Roll the composite sheet through the pasta machine at the thickest setting.

6 Fold the sheet in half so the same colors meet (below, left). Roll the sheet through the pasta machine, folded edge first.

7 Continue to fold the sheet in the same direction and roll it through the machine until there are smooth gradations with no lines.

TIPS FOR REDUCING CANES

- Firm, general-use clays will retain detail better when used to create canes.
- Canes must be pliable and warm to be reduced and formed into shapes.
- Prevent older canes from cracking during reduction by coating them with a small amount of liquid clay prior to warming.
- Warm your canes by placing them on a heating pad set on the lowest setting. Check the canes often to make sure they do not overheat.
- Wear latex gloves to avoid transferring fingerprints to the clay.

Adding a patina

Get a beautiful, colorful patina using liver of sulfur, a nontoxic solution. Because liver of sulfur has a strong odor, use it in a well-ventilated area. Place a small chunk of liver of sulfur in a small cup of hot water and let dissolve. Use tweezers to dip your metal clay piece into the solution; when you like the color, remove it and rinse with cold running water. Use a polishing cloth or pad to remove some of the patina.

Working with metal clay

You can combine polymer and metal clay in one piece for truly stunning results. Many of the techniques and tools are similar; if you're comfortable with polymer clay, it will be easy to work with metal clay.

Metal clay dries rapidly, so remove only the amount you will use during a given work session. Store unused clay in an airtight container with a small piece of moist sponge or paper towel. Cover clay with plastic wrap while you are not working with it. Use a spray bottle to remoisten the clay if it begins to dry out.

Apply olive oil or natural hand balm to your hands, tools, and work surface to prevent the clay from sticking. Decide how thick you want your metal clay sheet to be. Make two stacks of either playing cards, mat board, or thickness guides that equal that thickness.

Place the lump of clay on your work surface between the two even stacks. Roll the clay out to a uniform thickness, using an acrylic roller or PVC tube. Rotate the clay 90 degrees and roll it again.

Drying metal clay

Dry metal clay completely before firing, or it can crack and break. (Speed drying by using a mug warmer, griddle set on low, or food dehydrator, if desired.)

Firing and polishing

Use a small, digitally programmable kiln, Hot Pot, or Ultralite (tabletop kiln) to fire pieces according to the metal clay manufacturer's instructions. You can also torch-fire small pieces of metal clay using a butane torch.

When the metal clay is fired, it will have a white surface. Polish to reveal the silver beneath with a wire brush and soapy water. For faster results, use a rotary tumbler with stainless steel shot.

METAL CLAY THICKNESS GUIDE

MEASUREMENT	SLAT COLOR	PLAYING CARD(S)
.25mm	black	1
.5mm	yellow	2
.75mm	green	3
1.0mm	blue	4
1.5mm	red	6
2.0mm	purple	8

SAFETY BASICS

- To fire metal clay, you will need a kiln or butane torch. Use your kiln in a well-ventilated area.
- Follow manufacturers' instructions for programming your kiln and firing times and temperatures.
- All tools should be dedicated for nonfood use.
- Don't torch-fire metal clay pieces that have a core inclusion, such as cork or wood clay.
- Be sure to let a metal clay piece dry completely before firing it. Don't kiln-fire or torch-fire metal clay pieces that are not completely dry, as they may explode.

Jewelry techniques

Plain loop

1 Trim the wire or head pin ⅜ in. (1cm) above the top bead. Make a right angle bend close to the bead.
2 Grab the wire's tip with roundnose pliers. The tip of the wire should be flush with the pliers. Roll the wire to form a half circle. Release the wire.

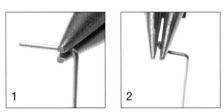

3 Reposition the pliers in the loop again and continue rolling.
4 The finished loop should form a centered circle above the bead.

Wrapped loop

1 Leave a 1¼-in. (3.2cm) wire tail. Grasp the wire with the tip of your chainnose pliers directly above the bead. Bend the wire (above the pliers) into a right angle.
2 Using roundnose pliers, position the jaws vertically in the bend.

3 Bring the wire over the top jaw of the roundnose pliers.
4 Keep the jaws vertical and reposition the pliers' lower jaw snugly into the loop. Curve the wire downward around the bottom of the roundnose pliers. This is the first half of a wrapped loop.

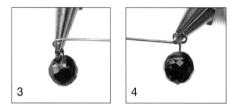

5 Position the chainnose pliers' jaws across the loop.
6 Wrap the wire around the stem, covering the stem between the loop and the top bead. Trim the excess wire and press the cut end close to the wraps with chainnose pliers.

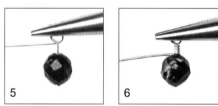

Flattened crimp

1 Hold the crimp using the tip of your chainnose pliers. Squeeze the pliers firmly to flatten the crimp.
2 Tug the wire to make sure the crimp is secure. If the wire slides, repeat the steps with a new crimp.

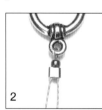

Folded crimp

1 Position the crimp bead in the notch closest to the crimping pliers' handle.
2 Separate the wires and squeeze the crimp.

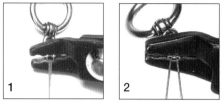

3 Move the crimp into the notch at the pliers' tip and hold the crimp as shown. Squeeze the crimp bead, folding it in half at the indentation.
4 Test that the folded crimp is secure.

Surgeon's knot

Cross the right end over the left end and go through the loop. Go through again. Pull the ends to tighten. Cross the left end over the right end and go through once. Pull the ends to tighten.

Overhand knot

Make a loop at the end of the thread. Pull the short tail through the loop, and tighten.

Square knot

Cross the left-hand end of the thread over the right, and bring it around and back up. Cross the end that is now on the right over the left, go through the loop, and pull both ends to tighten.

Projects

Domestic diva

Stamp words and vintage images onto polymer clay tiles

designed by **Lori Wilkes**

supplies:

bracelet, 8 in. (20cm)

- polymer clay in each of **7** colors:
  - ¼ oz. black
  - 3 oz. cadmium yellow
  - ¼ oz. gold
  - 1¼ oz. green
  - 1½ oz. red
  - 1½ oz. turquoise
  - 1½ oz. white
- **14** 4mm round glass beads
- **2** crimp beads
- 1 yd. (.9 m) .7mm stretch jewelry fiber or elastic cord
- Big Eye needle
- acrylic paint, red and black
- acrylic roller
- clay extruder with square-hole disk
- flexible clay texture sheets
- acrylic floor finish
- buffing machine or electric drill with felt wheel and 2mm drill bit
- needle tool or piercing needles
- 1¼ x 1½-in. (3.2 x 3.8cm) oval cutter
- paintbrush
- paper towels
- pasta machine*
- scissors
- scrap paper (optional)
- tissue blade
- toaster oven*
- vintage rubber or metal plate stamps
- crimping pliers

*Dedicated to use with polymer clay

Protect your work surface by covering it with paper. Wash your hands every time you switch clay colors, and condition each block of clay.

Clay tiles

Checkerboard sheet

1 Make olive-colored clay: Combine 1 oz. cadmium yellow and ¼ oz. each of green and gold. Mix the colors together until blended with no visible streaks.

2 Make creamy yellow clay: Combine 1 oz. cadmium yellow and ½ oz. white. Mix the colors together until blended with no visible streaks.

3 Place the disk with the square-shaped hole into the cap of the clay extruder. Put the olive-colored clay in the clay extruder, and expel all of the clay from the extruder. Cut the clay into six 4½-in. (11.4cm) lengths. Repeat with the creamy yellow clay.

4 Stack the lengths of clay, alternating colors to form a checkerboard pattern: Place olive, creamy yellow, then olive in the first row. Place creamy yellow, olive, then creamy yellow in the second row. Repeat the first and second row patterns for the third and fourth rows **(photo a)**. Press the clay together, and use an acrylic roller to remove air bubbles.

5 Set the pasta machine to a middle setting, and roll the remaining creamy yellow clay through it to make a sheet that is 3½ x 4½ in. (8.9 x 11.4cm).

6 Using a tissue blade, cut even, thin slices of checkerboard cane, and apply them carefully to the yellow sheet, leaving no space between the slices and lining them up to continue the alternating checkerboard pattern **(photo b)**.

7 Use an acrylic roller to remove air bubbles. Set the pasta machine to the thickest setting, and roll the checkerboard sheet through it. Reduce the setting by one, and roll the sheet through it. Reduce the setting again, and roll the sheet through it.

Interior stacks

1 Make dark red clay: Combine 1½ oz. red and ¼ oz. black. Mix the

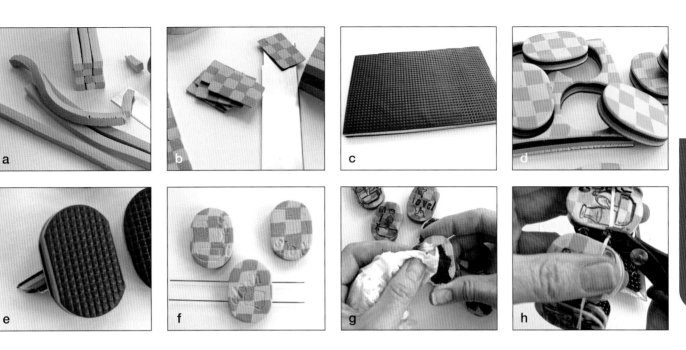

a

b

c

d

e

f

g

h

colors together until blended with no visible streaks.

2 Make yellow-green clay: Combine 1 oz. each of cadmium yellow and green. Mix the clay together until it is blended with no visible streaks.

3 Set the pasta machine to the thickest setting, and roll the dark red clay through it. Trim the sheet to 3½ x 6 in. (8.9 x 15cm).

4 Repeat step 3 with the yellow-green clay and the turquoise clay.

5 Stack the sheets with the dark red clay on the bottom, the turquoise clay in the middle, and the yellow-green clay on top.

6 Set the pasta machine to a thin setting, and roll the remaining dark red clay through it. Trim the sheet to 3½ x 6 in. (8.9 x 15cm). Increase the setting to the next thickness. Place the texture sheet on top of the clay sheet, and run the clay and texture sheets together through the pasta machine. Stack the textured clay on top of the yellow-green clay, and gently press the clay with an acrylic

roller to remove air bubbles. Trim the edges of the stacks **(photo c)**.

7 Turn over the stack, and place the checkerboard sheet on top of the stack. Gently press the clay stack with an acrylic roller to remove air bubbles.

Finishing

1 Using the oval cutter, cut out seven or eight tiles **(photo d)**.

2 Create a slight bevel on the long edges of the tiles: With the checkerboard side facing up, use the tissue blade to trim the edge with a slight slant toward the inside of the tile. From the back of the tile, you will be able to see the layers **(photo e)**.

3 Using various vintage rubber stamps or metal plates, press images and words into the surface of the checkerboard side of the tiles. Refine any light or distorted impressions with a needle tool. Using the needle tool or piercing needles, make two horizontal holes through the sides near the top and bottom of each tile **(photo f)**. (The needles can be baked in place.)

4 Following the clay manufacturer's instructions, bake the tiles in the toaster oven. Allow the tiles to cool completely. Remove the needles.

5 Mix a pea-sized portion each of red and black acrylic paint to make dark red paint. Paint the indentations from the stamps on the surface of each tile, and wipe off any excess paint with a damp paper towel **(photo g)**. Let the paint dry.

6 Carefully buff each tile with a buffing machine or an electric drill fitted with a

felt wheel. Using the drill bit, open the holes made in step 3, if needed. Wipe off excess clay dust.

7 Apply one coat of acrylic floor finish to each tile. Let dry. Apply a second coat to the image side of each tile. Let dry.

Assembly

1 Cut 18 in. (46cm) of stretch jewelry fiber or elastic cord. Thread a Big Eye needle to the center of the fiber or cord, and string a crimp bead and an alternating pattern of a 4mm round glass bead and a tile, going through the top hole until you've strung all the tiles.

2 Go through the crimp bead strung in step 1. Test the fit, and add or remove beads as needed. Pull the fiber or cord slightly snug to create a little tension. Crimp the crimp bead **(photo h)**. Trim the ends, and gently tug the fiber or cord to tuck the crimp bead inside a tile.

3 Repeat steps 1 and 2, going through the bottom holes of the tiles.

EDITOR'S NOTES:
Experiment with color! Choose colors that remind you of your mother's kitchen, or use colors that fit your current style. If you want a bigger bangle, make an eighth tile or add extra 4mm rounds between tiles.

DESIGNER'S NOTE:
If you do not have an extruder, run the first color through the pasta machine on the thickest setting. Cut the sheet to 1½ x 4½ in. (3.8 x 11.4cm). Repeat twice, creating a three-layer stack. Cut the stack into ¼-in. (6mm) strips. Repeat.

Extra chunky cuff

A bold cuff demands to be noticed. Textures and an image transfer personalize a polymer clay bracelet that makes a statement

designed by **Barbara A. McGuire**

Preparing the base

1 Condition each block of clay. Combine 2 oz. each of white and ecru. For a faux bone look, mix the colors until blended with no visible streaks. For a stone look, stop mixing before the colors are completely blended.

2 With the pasta machine set to the thickest setting, roll two 2 x 8-in. (5 x 20cm) strips of clay and one 1 x 8-in. (2.5 x 20cm) strip of clay. Lay the strips on the ceramic tile work surface.

3 Center the 1 x 8-in. (2.5 x 20cm) strip on top of a 2 x 8-in. (5 x 20cm) strip. Be sure to center the smaller strip evenly, as it will become the guide for

the channels through which the elastic cord will run.

4 Position the pony bead lacing along both sides of the center strip, creating a loop on one end **(photo a)**.

Image and texture

1 Select an area on the remaining 2 x 8-in. (5 x 20cm) strip to place the

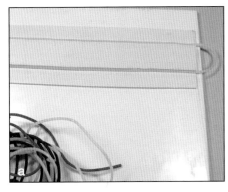

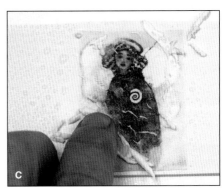

supplies:

bracelet, 7½ in. (19.1cm)

- polymer clay, 2 oz. each of **2** colors: white and ecru
- 35–45mm stone donut
- 6–10mm round accent bead (additional beads if necessary to adjust for length)
- coin bead with center hole or metal finding (optional)
- acrylic paint, raw umber
- assorted deep-impression stamps
- buffing machine
- burnisher or bone folder
- 8 x 8-in. (20 x 20cm) ceramic tile work surface
- 24 in. (61cm) clear elastic cord
- craft knife
- glue or G-S Hypo Cement (optional)
- liquid polymer
- spray bottle with water
- pasta machine*
- photocopy of image, sized to fit bracelet
- 24 in. (61cm) pony bead lacing
- soda can, glass, or cardboard tube about 2½ in. (6.4cm) diameter
- soft cloth rag
- stiff bristle paintbrush
- tissue blade
- toaster oven*
- water tray
- wet/dry sandpaper (320-, 400-, 600-grit)

*Dedicated to use with polymer clay

DESIGNER'S TIPS:

- **Images should be copyright free or used with permission.**
- **Images should be printed with a machine that uses toner, such as a color copier.**
- **Practice on a few scrap pieces of clay with extra copies of the image.**
- **When transferring the image, don't go overboard scraping away the paper. You can remove the paper later in the process, too, but I like to have the image fairly exposed before I continue.**
- **If you don't get a good transfer, turn the strip over or remake it and try again.**
- **If you get too much paint on the bracelet sections, you can remove it with rubbing alcohol.**

image. Lay the image face down on the clay, and use a burnisher or bone folder to burnish the image onto the clay **(photo b)**. Let the image set for a few minutes to bond the toner to the clay.

2 Spray the image with water to saturate the paper, and begin to shred the paper away from the clay with your fingertip until the image appears **(photo c)**. Do not scrub too hard or smear the image.

3 Mist a deeply etched stamp with water, and press it firmly into the remaining portions of the strip to emboss it **(photo d)**. Repeat with as many stamp patterns as you would like until the whole strip is decorated.

Shaping the bracelet

1 Coat the 1 x 8-in. (2.5 x 20cm) center strip and the edges of the 2 x 8-in. (5 x 20cm) bottom strip with liquid polymer, and place the decorated strip on top of the center and bottom strips **(photo e)**. Press evenly to attach the decorated strip to the middle and edges of the other strips. Use a burnisher or bone folder to smooth the edges

g

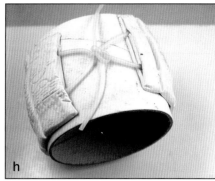

h

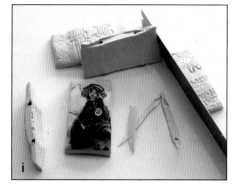

i

j

k

l

m

n

EDITOR'S NOTE:
The elastic cord may snap if it gets stretched too tightly. As you work, be sure to leave enough slack.

together. Trim the edges if desired (photo f).

2 Press the burnisher or bone folder into the bracelet at intervals to create sections (photo g). The pony bead lacing will prevent the tool from going all the way through. Use a tissue blade to scrape the bracelet from the work surface.

3 Bend the bracelet around the soda can, glass, or cardboard tube, and tie the ends of the pony bead lacing together temporarily to secure the shape (photo h). Smooth out any undesired cracks that may develop from bending. Coat the image with liquid polymer.

Baking and finishing

1 Following the polymer clay manufacturer's instructions, bake the bracelet in the toaster oven. Allow the

bracelet to cool completely, and remove it from the toaster oven.

2 Remove the bracelet from the form, and remove the lacing from the bracelet. Use a craft knife to cut the sections apart. Keep the sections in order so they don't get mixed up.

3 Use a tissue blade to trim the edges of each section (photo i), so they will be smooth where they will meet.

4 Paint the embossed sections with acrylic paint, and paint around the image but not over it. Remove most of the paint with a damp cloth rag (photo j).

5 Working from the roughest to smoothest grits, wet-sand each section except for the image transfer. Buff each section (photo k).

Bracelet assembly

1 Fold the elastic cord in half, and string the sections in order onto both ends of elastic cord. Leave a little slack for the folded end to work as a loop clasp (photo l). Remove sections or add beads at the end to adjust the length of the bracelet.

2 On both ends of the elastic cord, string a donut and, if desired, a coin or finding. Cross the ends through the accent bead (photo m). Slide the ends back through the coin or finding and donut.

3 Snug up the beads, and tie an overhand knot at the back of the donut (photo n). Tie a second overhand knot, allowing the double knot to nestle in the donut's hole. To keep the knot tied, add an optional dab of glue or G-S Hypo Cement, and let it dry.

supplies:

pendant, 1½ x 2¾ in.
(3.8 x 7cm)

- ½ oz. black polymer clay
- liquid polymer clay (optional)
- metal leaf foil (variegated)
- 6mm bicone crystal
- 4mm bicone crystal
- 4mm spacer
- 1½-in. (3.8cm) head pin
- 1½-in. (3.8cm) eye pin
- acrylic roller
- alcohol inks (optional)
- needle tool
- pasta machine*
- rubber or leather cord
- semi-gloss sealer
- soft paintbrush
- spray bottle with water
- superglue or two-part epoxy
- texture sheet
- tissue blade
- toaster oven*
- chainnose pliers
- roundnose pliers
- wire cutters

*Dedicated to use with polymer clay

Foiled again

Create a textured polymer clay pendant with variegated foil

designed by **Nancy Clark**

Pendant
Foiled clay shape

1 Condition the block of clay. Set the pasta machine to the thickest setting, and roll a sheet of clay about 1½ x 2¾ in. (3.8 x 7cm).

2 Spray the texture sheet with water, and place it on the clay. Using an acrylic roller, roll the texture sheet firmly over the clay, and remove the texture sheet. Gently dry the clay with a paper towel, or let it air-dry completely.

3 Place a piece of metal leaf foil on the clay sheet, and gently rub the foil onto it with the paintbrush. Be sure to press into the crevices so the foil is well attached. Some cracks in the foil will appear as part of the design **(photo a)**.

4 If desired, dab single drops of ink onto the foil in a random pattern, and let dry.

5 Using a tissue blade, cut the clay into the desired shape **(photo b)**.

6 To make the back of the pendant, repeat steps 1 and 2.

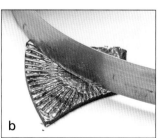

a

b

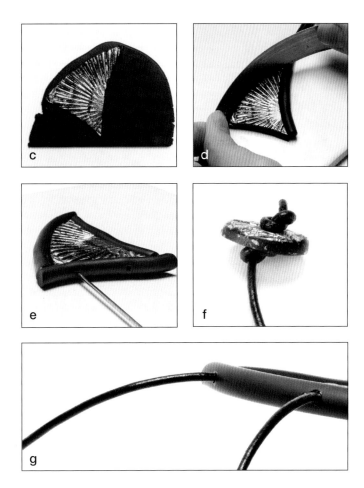

7 Place the textured side of the new sheet of clay face down, and place the foiled clay on top of it face up (photo c). If desired, apply a small amount of liquid polymer clay between the sheets. Trim the edges of the new sheet of clay even with the foiled clay.

8 To create a clasp bead from the scrap clay, cut a circle about ½ in. (1.3cm) in diameter, and use the needle tool to poke a hole through the center.

Pendant frame

1 Roll the remaining clay into a cylinder about ⅛–¼ in. (3–6mm) in diameter. Place the cylinder along an edge of the pendant, and trim the edges with the tissue blade (photo d). If desired, place a small amount of liquid polymer clay between the edge of the pendant and the cylindrical frame. Repeat on all sides, creating lap joints or mitered corners as desired.

2 Using the needle tool, make two holes about ¼ in. (6mm) deep along the edge of the top cylinder where you want the neck cord to attach (photo e). Using the eye pin, make another hole at the bottom of the pendant.

3 Following the clay manufacturer's instructions, bake the pendant and clasp bead in the toaster oven. Allow the pendant to cool completely. Following the manufacturer's instructions, add a coat of sealer.

Assembly

Neck cord

1 Cut the cord into two pieces half the desired length of the finished necklace.

2 On one cord, string the clasp bead, and tie an over-hand knot near the edge.

Snug the bead up to the knot, and tie another overhand knot after the bead (photo f).

3 On the other cord, make a loop large enough for the clasp bead to fit through, and tie an overhand knot.

4 Dot the remaining ends of the cords with glue, and insert them into the holes at the top of the pendant (photo g). Let dry.

Crystal dangle

1 On a head pin, string the crystals and spacer as desired. Make a wrapped loop.

2 Open the loop of the eye pin, attach the crystal dangle, and close the loop.

3 Trim the eye pin to fit in the hole at the bottom of the pendant. Apply glue to the eye pin, insert it into the bottom hole, and let dry.

DESIGNER'S NOTES:

- When cutting your shapes, you can either cut them free hand or draw a pattern and cut around it.
- I prefer to drill my holes after baking the clay. Choose a drill bit the same diameter as your cord and another one the same diameter as your eye pin. If the cord does not fit into the holes, use the drill to widen them.

Polymer pod pendant

Sew beads onto a polymer form to make a pod bursting with your favorite jewels

designed by **Tea Benduhn**

supplies:

pendant, 1½ x 2 in. (3.8 x 5cm)

- 2–3 oz. polymer clay in each of **1–2** colors
- **40–60** assorted drop beads and briolettes
- 2 in. (5cm) 20-gauge wire
- Fireline 6-lb. test
- beading needles, #10
- acrylic roller
- needle tool
- pasta machine*
- tissue blade
- toaster oven*
- wet/dry sandpaper (400-, 600-, 800-grit)
- roundnose pliers
- wire cutters

*Dedicated to use with polymer clay

Beaded dome

1 Condition each block of clay. Using any color clay, roll an egg-shaped ball about ½ x ¾ in. (1.3 x 1.9cm). Cup the ball in your palm, and press an indentation into the ball with your thumb, creating a dome shape ¼ in. (6mm) thick **(photo a)**.

2 Maintaining the curvature of the dome, press the pointed end of assorted drop beads and briolettes onto the convex surface of the dome, leaving about ⅛ in. (3mm) around the edges uncovered. Remove the beads, and use the needle tool to poke a hole through the center of each indentation created by a bead **(photo b)**. Following the clay

a

b

c

d

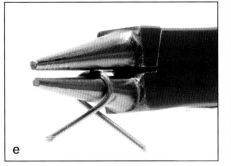

e

f

g

h

manufacturer's instructions, bake the dome in the toaster oven. Allow it to cool completely.

3 On 2 yd. (1.8m) of Fireline, leaving a 6-in. (15cm) tail, sew through a hole in the dome, back to front. Pick up a drop bead or briolette, and sew back through the hole your thread exited **(photo c)**. Sew up through an adjacent hole, pick up a drop bead or briolette, and sew back through the hole. Snug up the beads, and tie the working thread and tail together with a square knot. Sew up through an adjacent hole, and continue adding drop beads or briolettes to fill all the indentations. If there are gaps, fill them in by attaching a second bead through a nearby hole. Tie the working thread and tail together with a square knot, and trim them to about ½ in. (1.3cm).

Outer shell

1 Using any color clay, roll an egg-shaped ball about 1 x 1½ in. (2.5 x 3.8cm), and press the back of the dome onto it. Press some clay around the edges of the dome **(photo d)**.
2 Cut a 1-in. (2.5cm) piece of wire. Using roundnose pliers, bend the wire in half, and cross the tails of the wire, forming a shape like an awareness ribbon **(photo e)**. Insert the wire into the clay where you want the necklace to attach to the pendant, and press the clay

around the insertion point to cover the tails. Repeat with the remaining wire **(photo f)**. Bake the beaded clay component in the toaster oven. Allow it to cool completely.
3 Set the pasta machine to a middle setting, and roll a sheet of clay about 2 x 2½ in. (5 x 6.4cm). Center the baked shape on the sheet, and fold the clay up around the edges, allowing the wire loops to poke through the clay **(photo g)**. Smooth the areas around the loops. Roll another sheet 2 x 2½ in. (5 x 6.4cm), and cut it in half. Place the clay strips around the edges of the beaded dome, and trim the clay close to the beads **(photo h)**. Using your fingers and clay tools, shape the clay into an organic-looking pod shape, and smooth the seams of the clay to form the outer shell. Bake the clay pod again. Allow it to cool completely.
4 Using wet sandpaper in increasingly finer grits, sand the surface underwater until smooth.

DESIGNER'S NOTES:
To wear the pendant as a necklace, string coordinating beads or seed beads, and attach your strung work through the wire loops. Alternatively, stitch a rope with 11º seed beads, attach it to the pendant by sewing through the wire loops, and add embellishments to conceal the connection.

Lovely little lamb

Combining polymer clay and pearls—not a b-a-a-a-d idea.
This lamb is so cute you will want a whole flock

designed by **Christi Friesen**

Lamb

1 Condition each block of clay.
2 To mix the wool color, combine 1 oz. each of white and pearl. Blend in approximately ¼ oz. of ecru as in step 1.
3 To mix the color for the face and legs, combine ¼ oz. each of burnt umber, gold, and ecru. Adjust the color as desired: Use more ecru for a lighter color or more burnt umber for a darker color.
4 Roll a 1-in. (2.5cm) ball of the wool-color clay. Flatten slightly with your hands. Cut a 3-in. (7.6cm) piece of

16-gauge wire and place it across the ball ¼ in. (6mm) from the top edge. Press the wire into the clay slightly **(photo a)**. This wire will remain in the piece throughout the sculpting and baking process. Use the channel the wire leaves after you remove it for stringing your pendant on a necklace.
5 Roll four ¼-in. (6mm) balls of the face/leg-color clay. Shape the balls into snakes, tapering them slightly at one end. Flatten the opposite end by pressing onto the work surface to create the hoof **(photo b)**.

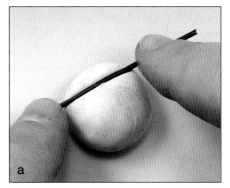

a

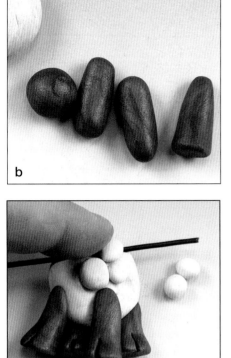

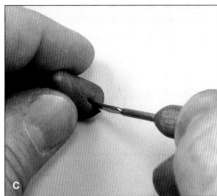

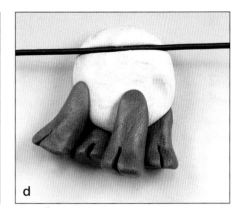

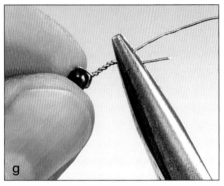

6 Stand each leg upright, and, using the sculpting tool, cut straight down to make a small notch on one side. Press into the cut with the sculpting tool to open the notch and smooth the opening for a more natural look **(photo c)**.

7 Attach the back legs to the body, pressing them into the back of the body, and leaving a little space between them. Turn the body over, and press firmly to smooth the connection between the body and the legs.

8 Attach the front legs, positioning them so that they alternate with the back legs. Pinch the tops of the front legs so they flatten where they attach to the body **(photo d)**.

9 Roll an assortment of small balls of the wool-color clay, varying the sizes. Gently press them onto the body, covering the 16-gauge wire, the tops of the front legs, and the visible parts of the belly. Press firmly enough so they adhere, but don't flatten them. The balls should look round and fluffy **(photo e)**.

10 Roll a ball of face/leg-color clay approximately one-quarter the size of

the body. Form an oval shape, tapering one end slightly. Position the oval on the body near the top, centered above the front legs. Pressing with your thumbs, attach the head to the body. The indentations will become the eye sockets **(photo f)**.

11 Cut a 2-in. (5cm) piece of 28-gauge wire. Center a 3mm bead on the wire. Grip the wire ends with chainnose pliers ¼ in. (6mm) from the bead. Grip the bead with your fingers and twist the wires until the twist reaches the bead **(photo g)**. Cut the wire, leaving a ⅛–¼-in. (3–6mm) twisted tail. Make a second wired bead.

12 Press the wired beads, wire tail first, into the center of each indentation on the head. Push until the wires are concealed in the clay **(photo h)**.

13 Using the tip of the sculpting tool, make small slits in the end of the face.

Begin with a V for the nostrils, and then make another slit at the base of the V to form a Y. For the mouth, press a little curved line beneath the Y **(photo i)**.

14 Brush a light coating of mica powder on the tip of the nose **(photo j)**.

15 Wash your hands. Make more small balls of wool-color clay, and gently press them on the forehead, covering the entire top of the head **(photo k)**.

16 To make the ears, roll two teardrop-shaped pieces of face/leg-color

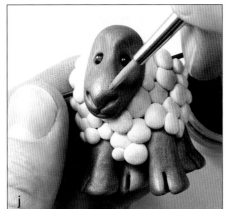

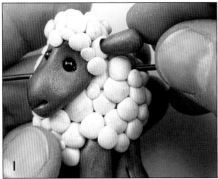

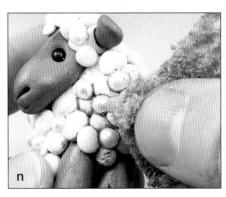

clay. Use the sculpting tool to make a hole in each side of the head. Press the teardrop-shaped pieces into the holes, (narrow end first). Press in firmly. Pinch the tops of the ears to flatten them **(photo l)**.

17 Repeat step 11 using pearls. Press them into the body, positioning them as desired **(photo m)**.

Baking and finishing

1 Bake the pendant according to the clay manufacturer's instructions.
2 Allow the piece to cool completely. After cooling, use chainnose pliers to remove the 16-gauge wire, pulling and twisting to loosen the wire if it sticks.
3 Using a paintbrush, apply a small amount of light-brown paint to the lamb, and immediately wipe it off with a damp sponge **(photo n)**. Use several sponges so that the remaining paint on the lamb does not become muddy. Allow the paint to dry completely.

4 Following the manufacturer's instructions, apply the clear coating or varnish. Do not paint over the pearls or the eyes.
5 Bake the lamb again to set all the finishes.

DESIGNER'S NOTES:
- **Wash your hands every time you switch clay colors, or the residue will mix with the other colors.**
- **Turn this lamb into a ram by twisting narrow teardrops into horns to replace the ears, and leaving more space between the legs. Small pieces of fiber can be added to create a shaggier look (see photo on page 21).**

supplies:
pendant
- polymer clay
  - 2 oz. each of **3** colors: white, ecru, and pearl
  - 1 oz. each of **2** colors: gold and burnt umber
- 12 4–5mm white or cream pearls
- 2 3–4mm beads
- 3 in. (7.6cm) 16-gauge craft wire
- 28 in. (71cm) 28-gauge craft wire
- clear coating or varnish
- red or pink mica powder
- toaster oven
- acrylic paint, light brown
- paintbrush (optional)
- pasta machine (optional)*
- sculpting tool
- sponges
- chainnose pliers

*Dedicated to use with polymer clay

Catch a wave

Dive into an improvised approach to making polymer clay color blends

designed by **Christi Friesen**

The harmonious hues and wavy shapes in this piece are all about the unpredictable nature of the ocean surf. For optimal results, remain open to surprises as you mix colors, sculpt the clay, and assemble the pieces to make this brooch.

Make color blends

1 Run white clay through your pasta machine on the thickest setting, and then lay chunks of green and blue clay on top of the white clay **(photo a)**. Without folding it, run the clay through the pasta machine again. Keeping the most interesting portion of the blend on the outside, fold the clay as in a Skinner blend, and run it through the pasta machine **(photo b)**. If the outer edges of the clay become ragged, trim them, and continue to fold the clay and run it through the pasta machine until you achieve a blend that you like **(photo c)**.
2 Repeat step 1 to make another blend. For a slightly different effect, make an accordion fold in the clay before running it through the pasta machine **(photo d)**.
3 Repeat step 1 to make a third blend, using the darker colors sparingly so that the final blend will provide a contrast to the first two blends **(photo e)**. To make a

a

more advanced blend, see "Make a Mokume Gane Pattern," p. 26.

Make the waves

1 Select one of the darker blends, and roll the clay into a snake so that the entire blend is visible **(photo f)**. Cut the snake to the desired length of one of your main waves, and then taper one end of the snake to a dull point. Make a rounded shape on the opposite end. Use a wooden sculpting tool or your finger to smooth the raw seam of cut clay **(photo g)**. Curl the rounded end of the snake. Use a pointed tool to define the eye of the curl **(photo h)**. Holding your blade at an angle, slice a bit of clay off the tapered end to reveal the pattern within the clay **(photo i)**. Smooth the cut end with your fingers.

Repeat with the other two color blends to make two more waves that are slightly smaller than the first one.

2 Arrange and connect the waves: Nest the smaller dark wave inside the curve of the large dark wave. Press the waves firmly together, and flatten them slightly **(photo j)**. Use a shaping tool to make indentations at the uncurled end of the outer wave **(photo k)**. Add the third wave, pressing it into the first two **(photo l)**.

3 Insert the focal pearl: Cut a 1½-in. (38mm) piece of 28-gauge craft wire. Center a 10mm pearl on the wire. Use pliers to hold the wires. With your other hand, turn the pearl until the wires twist tightly against it **(photo m)**. Use pliers to make a U shape in the wires **(photo n)**. Insert the wire U into the tip of the waves **(photo o)**. If necessary, secure the pearl by adding a small pinch or two of clay to the back of the piece.

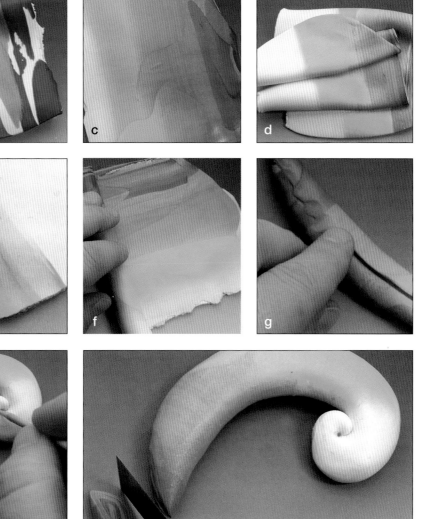

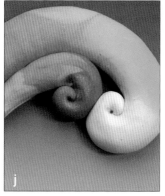

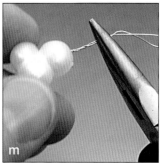

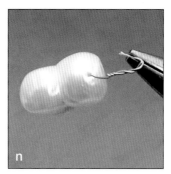

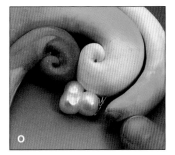

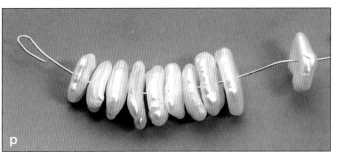

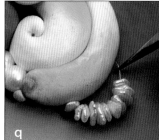

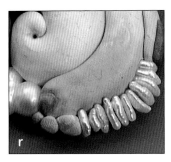

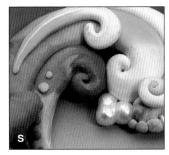

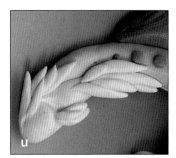

4 Add smaller pearls and clay details. Cut a 3-in. (7.6cm) piece of 28-gauge craft wire. Using roundnose pliers, make a U bend ½ in. (1.3cm) from one end of the wire. String 5mm pearls on the other end of the wire **(photo p)**. Make another U bend after the pearls.

5 Use needlenose tweezers to insert one wire end into the wide end of the outer wave. Press the pearls into the clay, and then insert the other wire end into the wave **(photo q)**.

6 Roll small clay balls, and press them against the wave and pearls to conceal any exposed wire **(photo r)**. Accentuate the curves in the design by adding a couple more small waves and dots of clay **(photo s)**.

7 Shape the fish: Make a teardrop shape with a small amount of white clay. Using a shaping tool, press an indentation for the gill ridge near the rounded end of the teardrop. Nest the fish shape against the tip of the inner wave, and press firmly **(photo t)**. Build the fins with rice-shaped pieces of rolled clay **(photo u)**. Use a pointed

MAKE A MOKUME GANE PATTERN:

Create more complex color blends of polymer clay using mokume gane, a layering technique borrowed from Japanese metalsmiths. You can cut wafer-thin pieces of clay from the resulting blends and use the blends as the ocean waves of the brooch.

1 Make clay strips: Condition four or five colors of clay that resemble the colors of an ocean wave. Run each color through a pasta machine on the widest setting. Cut the slabs into strips.

2 Stack and fuse the strips: Alternating the colors, stack the strips. Run the stack through the pasta machine on the widest setting. Fold and rerun the strips through the pasta machine three times. You will have a slab of clay made of very thin layers of color.

3 Roll and cut the waves: Roll the slab of clay. Using a tissue blade, cut thin slivers from the tapered end of the wave to reveal the ringed pattern. Once you have a pattern you like, gently smooth the cuts, being careful not to blur the delicate lines of clay. Make additional wave pieces using this technique.

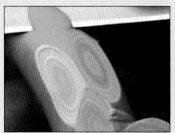

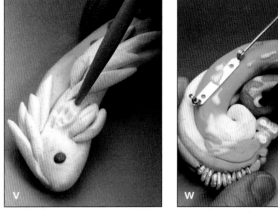

v

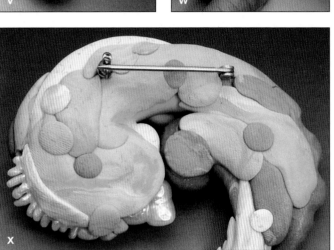

w

x

Process photos by Christi Friesen

ADD A PATINA:

After you have baked your piece the second time, allow it to cool. Follow these steps to add a patina to your brooch:

1 Use a dry paintbrush to apply a coat of acrylic paint to a small area of the brooch **(photo a)**.

2 Dip a sponge in water and rinse it. Then, wipe away most of the paint. Leave just enough paint to emphasize the textures and details of the brooch **(photo b)**.

3 Repeat steps 1 and 2 until you have added the desired amount of patina.

4 Protect the patina with a coat of polymer clay clear, satin sealer. Use a paintbrush to apply sealer to the front. Dry the piece, and then repeat on the back **(photo c)**. Bake the piece according to the clay manufacturer's instructions.

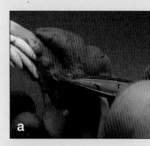

a

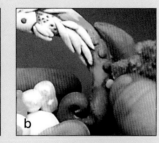

b

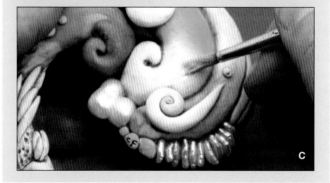

c

tool to make a depression for the eye. Press a small ball of clay into the depression. Suggest scales by pressing small lines into the body of the fish **(photo v)**.

8 Bake the piece on cardstock according to the clay manufacturer's instructions. When the piece is cool, dab liquid polymer clay on the back of an open pin-back finding. Press the pin back onto the back of the brooch.
9 Dab liquid clay on top of the pin back, avoiding the hinge and catch. Also dab liquid clay in any areas that need to be stabilized **(photo w)**, including any seams that need reinforcing and the line of 5mm pearls along the outside of the wave.
10 Make thin disks of clay to cover these dabs of liquid clay. Apply a thin layer of liquid clay to each disk, and

press the disks over the dabs of liquid clay. On the pin back, be careful to keep clay out of the hinge and catch **(photo x)**.
11 Turn the brooch over to make sure that none of the clay on the back is visible from the front. Bake the piece again. If you want to emphasize the textures in the brooch, add a patina with acrylic paint. See "Add a Patina," above.

EDITOR'S NOTE:
Adopt a freestyle attitude! The goal with color blends for this application is to invite a little chance, not to aim for a precise variegation. This is a slight departure from a traditional Skinner blend, which strives to make a seamless transition between colors.

supplies:

eight beads: four large, four small
- polymer clay
  - 2 oz. black
  - 2 oz. turquoise
  - 1 oz. white
  - 1 oz. translucent
- 5 x 5-in. (13 x 13cm) sheet gold, silver, copper, or variegated metal leaf
- Piñata Ink, brown
- Piñata Claro Extender (optional)
- neutral shoe polish
- bamboo skewer or needle tool
- nonstick work surface
- toaster oven*
- parchment paper
- pasta machine*
- small paintbrush
- soft cloth
- spray bottle with water
- texture sheet or texture tools
- tissue blade
- wet/dry sandpaper (1500 grit)

*Dedicated to use with polymer clay

Spirit of the Southwest

Re-create the red clay landscapes and abundant turquoise of Santa Fe in easy, lightweight polymer clay beads. Metal leaf and pigment bring an old-world feel to contemporary materials

designed by **Pam Wynn**

Beads

1 Condition 2 oz. of black polymer clay. Using a pasta machine on its thickest setting, roll the clay into a sheet.

2 Gently place a sheet of metal leaf on top of the black clay **(photo a)** and smooth out any air bubbles with your fingers.

3 Condition 1 oz. of translucent clay. Using the pasta machine on its thickest setting, roll the clay into a sheet. Gradually adjusting the machine to thinner settings, continue rolling until the clay is quite thin but still workable. My final pass was the seventh setting. If you find your sheet rippling, run it through sandwiched between two sheets of parchment paper.

4 Place the translucent clay onto the leafed black clay

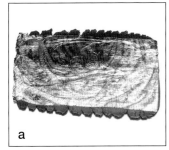

a

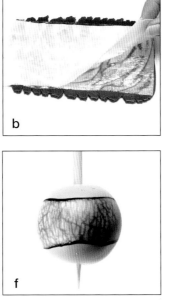

b

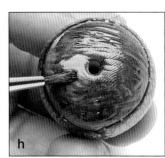

c

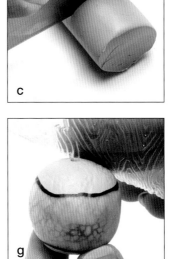

d

e

f

g

h

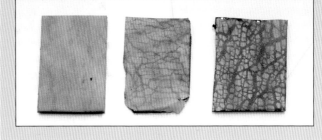

i

(photo b). Roll the leafed black-and-translucent sheet through the pasta machine on the thickest setting. Roll a few more times, changing to the next-thinnest setting to remove any air bubbles. Trim away the jagged edges, and set aside.

5 Condition 2 oz. of turquoise clay and 1 oz. of white clay. Run them through the pasta machine together several times until they are well blended.

6 Roll the turquoise-and-white mixture into a snake approximately 6 in. (15cm) long. Use a tissue blade to cut off a 1-in. (2.5cm) piece (photo c). Roll the piece into a ball between your palms.

7 Cut a ¼–½-in. (6–13mm) strip of the leafed black clay, and wrap it around the turquoise ball (photo d). Overlap the ends if you like, or leave a bit of turquoise bead showing between them. Roll the ball between your palms until the strip is flat and fused to the turquoise ball (photo e).

8 Make a hole in the bead with a needle tool or bamboo skewer (photo f).

9 Spray a texture sheet with water, and gently press it into the turquoise areas of the bead randomly (photo g).

10 Repeat steps 6–9 to make three more large beads. To make the small beads, repeat four more times, but cut only ½ in. (1.3cm) from the snake in step 6. If desired, make different textures and designs by varying the placement of the leafed black strips and using different texture tools.

11 To prevent the beads from flattening out as they bake, make a paper fan with parchment paper and place the beads within the folds before baking. Bake the beads according to the clay manufacturer's instructions.

12 When the beads are cool, use a small paintbrush to paint the turquoise portions of the beads with Piñata Ink (photo h). Let them dry.

13 Lightly sand a little of the ink off with 1500-grit sandpaper. If the color is not quite what you want, apply a thinned solution of ink (thinned with Piñata Claro Extender) to the bead and immediately blot the excess. Sand again if desired.

14 Apply a tiny amount of neutral shoe polish, and buff with a soft cloth (photo i).

EDITORS' NOTE:
As you run a sandwiched metal leaf sheet through your pasta machine, the metal leaf develops more crazing and the top layer becomes more transparent, as shown. To make these samples, we covered the leafed black clay with translucent clay that had been rolled out on the fifth setting. We then rolled the entire sheet on the thickest setting (left), the second-thickest setting (middle), and the third-thickest setting (right). If you like a lot of crazing but also want the look of a deep translucent layer, start with a thicker sheet of translucent clay.

SHAPING

It's good to be king

Embellish a polymer clay lion with pearls and gemstone beads for a truly royal pendant

designed by **Christi Friesen**

supplies:

one lion pendant

- polymer clay
  - 2 oz. ecru
  - 2 oz. gold
  - 2 oz. raw sienna
  - ½ oz. blue pearl
- **2** 5–6mm garnet beads
- **12–24** 5mm potato-shaped pearls, brown or silver
- **6–12** 5mm round carnelian beads
- 1–2 yd. (.9–1.8m) 28-gauge craft wire
- 4 in. (10cm) 14- or 16-gauge wire, or metal crochet hook
- Sculpey satin glaze or other clear varnish
- acrylic paint: burnt sienna, raw sienna, or burnt umber (optional)
- **2** index cards or cardstock
- craft knife or tissue blade
- flatnose or chainnose pliers
- needle tool
- paintbrush
- pasta machine*
- sponge (optional)
- toaster oven with baking sheet*
- wire cutters
- wooden clay-modeling tool*

*Dedicated to use with polymer clay

a

b

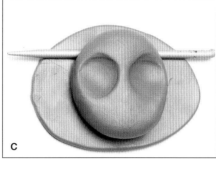

c

d

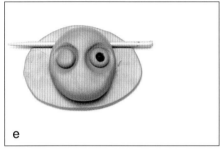

e

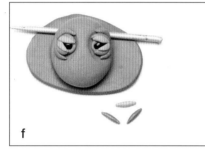

f

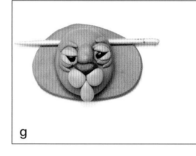

g

Prepare the clay

1 Condition the clay by running each color through the pasta machine on the widest setting.

2 Combine 1 oz. of ecru with ½ oz. each of raw sienna and gold to make the base color. Run the colors through the pasta machine several times. While the clay still has some streaks in it, cut off about one-third, and set it aside for the mane. Blend the remaining two-thirds thoroughly.

3 Cut two lima-bean-sized pieces of the base-colored clay. Lighten one by mixing it with a small amount of ecru. Darken the other by mixing it with a small amount of raw sienna. These are accent colors for the face.

4 Using the clay set aside in step 1 and small amounts of the accent colors, prepare small snakes of clay for the mane by twisting long pieces of clay together **(photo a)**. Fold the twisted clay, and twist it again. The more it is folded and twisted, the finer the streaks of color will be. When the streaks are well-distributed, break off small pieces, and twist them into 1-in. (2.5cm) snakes

(photo b). Make a lot of these so your lion can have a full mane. For a little variety, add a very small dab of blue pearl clay to some of the twists. A little blue goes a long way.

Make the head

1 Roll two approximately 1-in. balls of base clay. Flatten one slightly. Flatten the other, and run it through the pasta machine on the widest setting to make a flat oval. Place it on clean white cardstock.

2 Lay a 4-in. (10cm) piece of 14- or 16-gauge wire or a crochet hook across the oval, about ½ in. (1.3cm) from the top. This will hold open a channel for later stringing.

3 Place the slightly flattened ball on top of the oval, just covering the wire, and press firmly to attach. Make the eye sockets by indenting the clay with your index fingers **(photo c)**.

Add details

1 Roll two ¼-in. (6mm)-diameter balls of base clay. Press them into the eye sockets, flattening them.

2 Center a garnet bead on a 2-in. (5cm) piece of wire. Use pliers to twist the wire ends together until the wire twists firmly against the bead **(photo d)**. Trim the wire, leaving a ¼-in. tail. Press the wired bead into the eye socket about halfway into the clay **(photo e)**. Repeat with the other garnet bead.

3 Roll rice-shaped pieces of accent-colored clay, and position them around the eyes for character **(photo f)**.

4 Roll three ¼-in.-diameter balls of base or accent clay for the cheeks and chin. Keep the cheeks round as you press them in place. Shape the chin into a teardrop, and wedge the pointed end between the cheeks.

5 Make the nose with a small triangle of blue pearl clay—either straight from the package or blended with a little raw sienna for a more muted tone. Aim the point of the triangle toward the lion's chin, and flatten it as you press it in place. Make the bridge of the nose with a small wedge of base or accent clay, and press it in place **(photo g)**.

6 Make the mane with the twisted snakes. Coil one end of some before

h

i

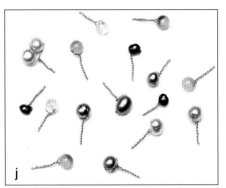

j

k

pressing them in place (photo h). Position them all around the lion's face, and layer them for fullness (photo i).

7 Make several rice-shaped pieces for the chin hair. Position them on the chin, and smooth them in with a wooden modeling tool.

Embellish and finish

1 Using the same method as for the eyes, make more wired-bead accents (photo j). This lion sports pearls and carnelian beads, but you may use whatever is in your bead supply. Sink the beads randomly into the mane (photo k).

2 Using the needle tool, texture the lion's cheeks.

3 Place the lion—still on the cardstock—on a baking sheet, and bake according to the clay manufacturer's instructions.

4 Let cool. While the clay is still warm, grasp one end of the wire or crochet hook with a pair of pliers, and remove it from the stringing hole by gently

twisting and pulling it. Let the lion cool completely.

5 Add an optional patina by applying acrylic paint to a small section with a dry brush. Then immediately wipe off the excess with a damp sponge so that paint remains only in the crevices and textured areas. Work quickly and carefully—acrylic dries fast.

6 Whether you opted for the patina or not, coat the clay with a clear, protective glaze. Place the lion on clean cardstock, and bake to set the glaze. Remove, and let cool.

Calling all calla lilies

A trio of trumpeting calla lilies makes a dramatic yet delicate bouquet to dangle from your neck

designed by **Christi Friesen**

Wash your hands every time you switch clay colors.

Mixing colors

1 Condition each block of clay. To mix the petal color, combine 1 oz. each of white and pearl. Blend in approximately ¼ oz. ecru, and mix the colors together until blended with no visible streaks.

2 To mix the stamen color, combine 1 oz. zinc yellow and ½ oz. ecru.

3 To mix the leaf color, combine 1 oz. each of gold and green pearl. As you blend the colors, leave some streaks for more earthy-looking leaves.

4 To mix the stem color, combine 1¼ oz. gold and 1 oz. green pearl.

5 To mix the red ribbon color, combine ⅓ oz. each of red pearl, gold, and ecru. If you'd rather have a blue ribbon, use blue pearl.

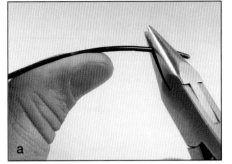

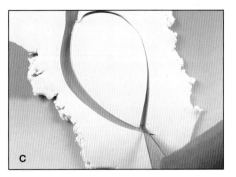

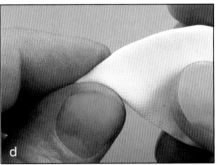

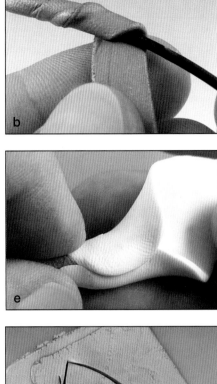

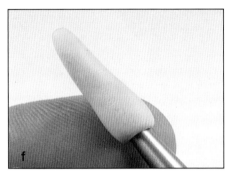

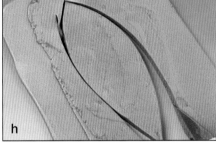

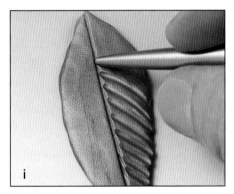

Sculpting the flower

1 Cut a piece of wire 2¼ in. (5.7cm) long, a piece 2 in. (5cm) long, and a piece 1¾ in. (4.4cm) long. Use chainnose pliers and your fingers to shape each wire into a gentle curve **(photo a)**.

2 Roll a snake of stem-colored clay about ¼ in. (6mm) in diameter and about 6 in. (15cm) long. Set the pasta machine to its third-thickest setting, and roll the snake lengthwise through the machine to make a ribbon of clay. Starting on one end of a piece of wire, wrap the clay diagonally around the wire **(photo b)**. Cut off any remaining clay, and shape the clay around the ends to cover the wire completely. Using your fingers or a dowel, smooth the clay around the wire to eliminate bumps and gaps. Repeat with the remaining wires to make a total of three stems.

3 Set the pasta machine to the second-thickest setting, and roll the petal-colored clay into a sheet about 2 x 3 in. (5 x 7.6cm). Referring to the figure on p. 35 as a guide, use a craft knife to cut a petal shape about 1½–2 in. (3.8–5cm) tall by ¾–1¼ in. (1.9–3.2cm) wide **(photo c)**.

4 Gently pinch the edges around the petal shape to eliminate the sharp cut marks. Pinch the tip to make it thinner and slightly curved to one side to mimic the natural curve of a calla lily **(photo d)**.

5 Fold the rounded part of the petal around the tip of a stem, overlapping one side of the petal on top of the other side. Press the edge of the petal into the stem, and smooth the area where the petal and stem meet **(photo e)**.

6 Roll a snake of stamen-colored clay about ¼ in. (6mm) in diameter and 1 in. (2.5cm) long. Using a tissue blade, slice the snake to ¾ in. (1.9cm) long. Using a dowel or round-end tool, press an indentation into the cut end of the

stamen **(photo f)**. Slide the stamen into the flower petal, pressing the indented end onto the stem. Using a paintbrush, brush gold mica powder onto the stamen **(photo g)**.

7 Repeat steps 3–6 for two more flowers.

8 Set the pasta machine to the second-thickest setting, and roll the leaf-colored clay into a sheet about 1½ x 3 in. (3.8 x 7.6cm). Using a craft knife, cut a leaf shape that is about 1¼ x 2½ in. (3.2 x 6.4cm) **(photo h)**. Gently pinch the edges as in step 4.

9 Using a needle tool, impress a line down the center of the leaf. Create the look of veins by using a round-end tool to impress lines from the center line to the edges of the leaf **(photo i)**. Roll a snake of stem-colored clay about ⅛ in. (3mm) in diameter and 2½ in. (6.4cm) long, and gently press the snake into the center line of a leaf. Press your thumb

j

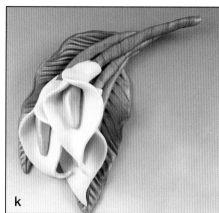

k

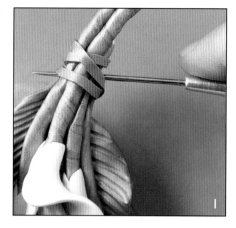

l

under the edges of the leaf to create a rippled look (photo j).

10 Repeat steps 8 and 9 to make a second leaf.

11 Place one leaf slightly overlapping the other, and press them together gently. Place the three flowers on top of the leaves, arranging the stack until you are pleased with the position of the flowers (photo k). Gently press the flowers, leaves, and stems together.

12 Set the pasta machine to the middle setting, and roll the ribbon-colored clay into a sheet about ¼ x 4 in. (6mm x 10cm). Use a craft knife to cut a strip of clay about ⅛ in. (3mm) wide. Wrap the clay ribbon around the stems lightly, criscrossing the ribbon over itself. Add a hole for stringing by using a needle tool to pierce the stems through the side (photo l).

Finishing

1 Set the lilies on a clean piece of paper, and follow the clay manufacturer's instructions to bake the clay flowers in the toaster oven. Allow the flowers to cool completely.

2 To create a patina, use the acrylic paint to paint a small area of the stems and leaves, then wipe off the surface paint with a sponge until very little color is left in the cracks (photo m). Repeat until you have added patina to the whole surface of the stems and leaves. Let the paint dry, and coat the whole surface of the flower, stems, and leaves with a clear, low-gloss varnish. Let the varnish dry.

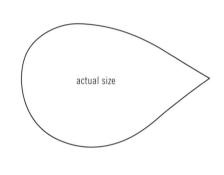

actual size

m

DESIGNER'S NOTES:
- **To make a brooch, use liquid polymer clay to attach a pin back to the back of the leaves, and cut a small strip of leaf-colored clay to lay over the attached portion of the pin back. Bake, following the clay manufacturer's instructions.**
- **Try replacing the stamen with an end-drilled stick pearl. Cut 1 in. (2.5cm) of 28-gauge craft wire, string it through the pearl's hole, and twist the wire. Cut the wire to leave ¼ in. (6mm), and bend the end to make a fishhook. Instead of the stamen, press the wire into the flower in "Sculpting the flower," step 6.**

supplies:
pendant, 2 x 4 in. (5 x 10cm)
- polymer clay
  - 1 oz. blue or red pearl
  - 2 oz. each of **6** colors: white, pearl, ecru, zinc yellow, green pearl
  - 3 oz. gold
- acrylic paint: burnt sienna or raw sienna
- clear varnish
- craft knife
- 6 in. (15cm) 16- or 18-gauge craft wire
- dowel or round-end tool
- mica powder: Aztec gold (PearlEx)
- needle tool
- pasta machine*
- soft paintbrush
- sponge
- tissue blade
- toaster oven*
- chainnose pliers
- wire cutters

*Dedicated to use with polymer clay

Bandana patterns

Use bright colors and translucent spirals to give
polymer clay the look of fabric

Designed by **Cassy Muronaka**

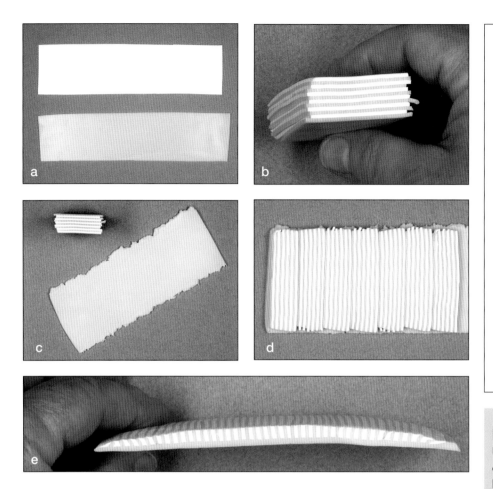

supplies:

24–30 beads, ⅞-in. (22mm) diameter
- polymer clay
  - 1 oz. white
  - 1 oz. translucent
  - 20 oz. your choice of colors
- 9 in. (22.9cm) elastic cording, ¹⁄₁₆-in. (1.5mm) diameter
- superglue
- pasta machine*
- tissue blade
- acrylic roller
- smoothing tool (optional)
- plastic bags
- circle cutter: ¾-in. (19mm) diameter
- nonstick work surface
- needle tool
- knitting needle (optional)
- toaster oven*

*Dedicated to use with polymer clay

DESIGNER'S NOTE:
Use the following formulas to create the colors shown in this bracelet:

```
   1 part cadmium red
+ 1 part zinc yellow
+ ⅛ part raw sienna
= tomato red

   1 part fuchsia
+ 1 part purple
+ 3 parts white
= light purple

   1 part cobalt blue
+ 1 part cadmium yellow
= forest green

   1 part burnt umber
+ 1 part raw sienna
+ 3 parts white
= beige

   1 part cobalt blue
+ 3 parts white
= sky blue

   1 part green
+ 1 part zinc yellow
= apple green
```

The wild fabrics that are strutted on fashion runways inspired this colorful polymer clay project. Translucent and white clays are artfully combined to make a striped spiral cane. Thin slices of the cane are then layered over bright clay blends. The curing process yields a finished bead that looks like soft cotton.

Make the cane

1 Condition the white and translucent clays. Roll out 1 oz. of white clay and run it through the pasta machine set to the medium-thin setting. Continue to run the clay through the machine until the clay is approximately 2½ x 9 in. (6.4 x 23cm). Use a tissue blade to trim the ragged edges of the clay. Repeat with 1 oz. of translucent clay **(photo a)**.
2 Lay the sheet of white clay flat on your work surface. Use a tissue blade to cut the sheet across its width into six equal pieces. Repeat with the translucent clay. Stack the clay pieces, alternating the translucent pieces with the white ones **(photo b)**.

3 Roll out the remaining 1 oz. of translucent clay and run it through the pasta machine set to the thickest setting **(photo c)**.
4 Cut ⅛-in. (3mm) slices from the 2-in. (51mm) ends of the clay stack. Lay the slices flush against each other on the slab of translucent clay **(photo d)**. Continue placing slices to the end of the translucent slab.
5 Without distorting the stripes, use an acrylic roller to smooth and level the surface of the clay. Trim the ragged edges of the clay strip.
6 Use your fingers to pinch and thin the short ends of the strip. This makes it easier to roll the strip into a cane. Leave the middle of the strip thicker.
7 Make a beveled cut ⅛ in. (3mm) from one end of the strip. Measure ¼ in. (6.5mm) from the opposite end of the strip and make another beveled cut **(photo e)**.
8 Cold clay is difficult to roll, so warm the clay if necessary by placing it in a plastic bag and setting the bag in a bowl of warm water. Begin at the ⅛-in. (3mm) beveled end and carefully roll

CANING

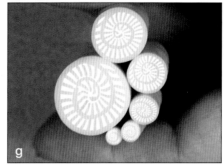

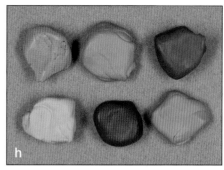
Process photos by Cassy Muronaka

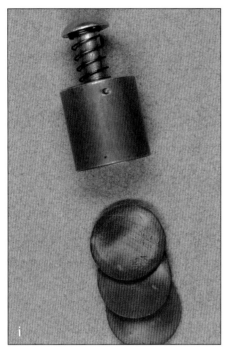

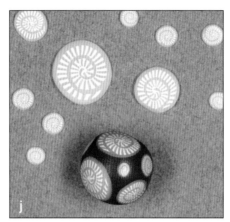

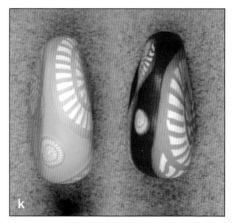

the strip into a jellyroll **(photo f)**. Smooth the seam with your fingers or a smoothing tool.

9 Use your hands to roll the cane to 5 in. (13cm) long. Cut the cane into two 2½-in. (6.4cm) long pieces. Set one piece aside. Roll the other piece to 5 in. long, and cut it in half. Reduce and cut the clay three more times to make a series of gradually smaller canes **(photo g)**.

10 Place the canes in a plastic bag and immerse the bag in a bowl of cool water. This firms up the clay and makes it easier to slice. Translucent clay is particularly pliable and susceptible to distortion when it's warm.

Make the beads

1 See "Color Blends," page 37, to mix the six colors used in the featured bracelet **(photo h)**. Or, select your own palette of solid colors. For a monochromatic effect, choose just one color or different values of the same color.

2 Separately run each color of clay through the pasta machine set to the medium-thick setting.

3 Use a ¾-in. (1.9cm) circle cutter to cut three circles from one slab of colored clay **(photo i)**. Combine the circles and roll them into a seamless ball. Repeat with all the colors until you have 24–30 balls.

4 Remove the canes from the plastic bag and place them on a nonstick work surface. Cut very thin slices from the canes. The thinner the slices, the more transparent the clay will appear after it is cured.

5 Lightly press a couple of large-diameter cane slices onto a clay ball, and then fill in the spaces with smaller slices in a random pattern **(photo j)**. Repeat until you've embellished all the clay balls.

6 Using your fingers, press each ball into a ⅜-in. (1cm)-thick lozenge. Further flatten one side of each lozenge to ¼-in. (6mm) thick **(photo k)**.

Make holes in the lozenges

1 Using a needle tool, make a hole in the center of each lozenge to fit your elastic cording. If necessary, use a knitting needle to enlarge the holes. In one bead, make the hole large enough to conceal a double knot of elastic cording.

2 Bake the beads in an oven according to the clay manufacturer's instructions.

3 Place the beads in a bowl of ice water to bring out the translucence of the clay. Dry the beads when they are cool.

Assemble the beads into a bracelet

Line up the beads so the thin edges of all the beads face the same direction. Place the bead with the large hole at one end. Cut an 8-in. (20cm) piece of elastic cording and thread it through the beads. Tie a double knot with the ends of the cording, and dab superglue on the knot. Trim the ends of the cording and pull the knot through the bead with the larger hole.

Tile pendant

Complex-looking polymer clay canes are easier to create than you might expect

designed by **Barbara Fajardo**

supplies:

pendant, 1¼ in. (3.2 cm) square
(materials make several)

- polymer clay
  - 2 oz. black
  - 1 oz. each of **4** colors: 2 light, 2 dark
- liquid polymer clay
- ¾in. (1.9cm) 20-gauge wire
- acrylic roller
- buffing pads (optional)
- ceramic tile (optional)
- chainnose pliers
- superglue
- pasta machine*
- sandpaper (optional)
- sharp tissue blade
- stylus tool (optional)
- toaster oven*
- unlined index cards or cardstock
- wire cutters

*Dedicated to use with polymer clay

Patterned cane

1 Condition all the clays. Set the black clay aside.

2 Working with one light color and one dark color, make a Skinner blend. Make a second blend with the remaining two colors.

3 Roll one blend into a jellyroll cane from dark to light. Repeat with the other blend, rolling from light to dark (**photo a**). Roll tightly to avoid trapping air bubbles in the clay.

4 Run half of the black clay through the pasta machine on the thinnest setting. Wrap each jellyroll cane in black clay (**photo b**). Do not overlap the edges of the black clay. Reduce the canes to ⅜–½ in. (1–1.3cm) in diameter by gently rolling them evenly against your work surface. Or, starting from the center, gently squeeze and pull the canes until they reach the desired diameter. Press out any air bubbles.

5 Make a cylinder about the same size with black clay only.

6 Using a tissue blade, cut the canes and cylinders into 2-in. (5cm) pieces (**photo c**).

7 Compress the pieces in different ways to make irregular or teardrop shapes (**photo d**).

8 Gather the pieces to form a rough triangle (**photo e**). As you create your pattern, place each pieces so its position is consistent from one end of the triangle to the other. With your fingers and work surface, press the bundle into a smooth triangle (**photo f**). Reduce the triangle to ¾ x 8 in. (1.9 x 20cm) by pushing the cane against your work surface and stretching it at the same time. Run your fingers along the sides to smooth out any lumps. Flip the cane from side to side and end to end,

and keep the diameter the same on each end.

9 Cut the cane into four equal parts. Place two triangles side by side so they mirror each other (**photo g**). Press the triangles together gently. This will give you a diamond shape. Repeat with the other two triangles, but choose a different side to align so you get a different pattern (**photo h**).

10 Hold the top corner (an obtuse angle) of one diamond, and flatten the other corner by pressing it against your work surface to form a new triangle. Repeat with the other diamond (**photo i**).

11 Position the triangles so the edges that were flattened on the work surface are against each other. Press them together to form a square.

12 Cut the cane in half crosswise, and place the two pieces side by side. Using an acrylic roller, reduce the new cane (**photo j**) to about 1 x ½ in. (2.5 x 1.3cm).

13 Cut the cane in half again (**photo k**), and assemble all four pieces into a square, facing mirrored edges toward each other. Gently run the acrylic roller over all sides of the cane to hold it together. Let the cane rest 15–20 minutes.

Pendant

1 With a tissue blade, cut a ⅛-in. (3mm) slice from the cane. To make sure the surface is even, slice across any high points on the tile with a tissue blade (**photo l**).

2 Roll a small amount of black clay through the pasta machine on the thickest setting. Place the cane slice on the black clay, and press gently to remove any air bubbles. Use the tissue blade to cut around the slice

k

l

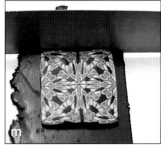

m

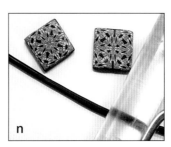

n

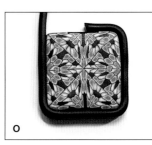

o

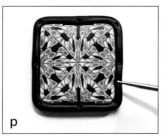

p

q

r

s

(photo m). If you wish, gently bevel the edges of the layered slice with your fingers or the acrylic roller.

3 Put the slice between two index cards, and place a ceramic tile on top. The tile isn't necessary, but it will ensure that your piece bakes flat. Bake the piece according to the clay manufacturer's instructions. Let it cool. Sand and buff it if desired.

4 Roll a ⅛-in.-diameter black snake to 5 in. (13cm) long. Gently flatten it with an acrylic roller (photo n).

5 Apply a thin bead of liquid polymer clay to the sides of your tile, and wrap the snake around the tile (photo o). Cut the snake at the top of the tile where the ends meet, and smooth the seam.

6 With a stylus, decorate the frame if desired (photo p).

7 Make a plain loop at the end of a ¾-in. piece of wire.

Roll a ¼-in. (6mm) ball of black clay (photo q).

8 Press the ball onto the top center of your pendant. Sink the straight end of the wire into the ball (photo r).

9 Using leftover black clay, decorate the frame if desired. Some embellishments to try include spirals, twists, crescents, leaves, and circles (photo s).

10 Bake the pendant again. Let it cool. Remove the wire loop, dab the end of it with glue, and reinsert it.

Make waves with cane slices

Shape polymer clay
in a fresh way to
form a dimensional
brooch

designed by
Jana Roberts Benzon

supplies:

brooch, 2 x 1½ in. (5 x 3.8cm),
15/16 in. (2.4cm) high

- polymer clay
  - 2 oz. white
  - 2 oz. dark brown
  - 2 oz. gold
- mica powder: gold
- pin-back finding
- liquid polymer clay
- stone or glass beads, sea shells
  (optional)
- pasta machine*
- latex gloves
- tissue blade
- craft knife
- smoothing tool or knitting needle
- dust mask
- soft, fine-tip paintbrushes
- unlined index cards
- acrylic block
- ceramic tile
- toaster oven*
- small cardboard box to fit in oven
- tweezers
- two-part epoxy
- toothpick

*Dedicated to use with polymer clay

EDITOR'S NOTE:
**You can wear latex gloves or
finger cots so you don't transfer
fingerprints to the clay.**

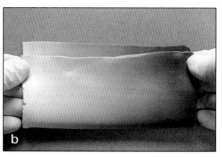

Instead of using polymer clay cane slices as flat elements in your designs, try using them as dimensional modular components. One advantage to making jewelry with modular components is that it's easy to create multiple pieces or to improvise on a theme. Another plus: Modular components challenge you to use repetition without becoming predictable. To make this brooch, you'll make a Skinner blend and build a lace cane. Then you'll shape lace-cane slices into dimensional pieces and arrange the pieces into a unified whole.

Make the can

1 Condition white, gold, and dark brown polymer clay.
2 Make a Skinner blend with the brown and white clays, starting with a 5 x 6-in. (13 x 15cm) clay rectangle **(photo a)**. Your Skinner blend doesn't need to be perfect for this project. Don't worry if the clay triangles are a bit irregularly shaped.

3 When your blend has an even color gradation, fold the clay in half, keeping the light ends together **(photo b)**. Starting with the dark end of the blend, run the clay through the pasta machine set to its thickest setting. Using the next four or five consecutively thinner settings, continue to run the blend through the pasta machine, creating a long, narrow sheet of clay.

NOTE: As the sheet lengthens, make sure that the clay doesn't fold back and stick to itself; this would make the sheet unusable for this project.

4 Use a tissue blade to trim the ragged edges from the light and dark ends of the sheet **(photo c)**.
5 Starting at the light end of the blend, roll the sheet into a cane, being careful not to trap any air bubbles between the layers of clay as you roll up the sheet **(photo d)**.
6 Run the conditioned gold clay through the pasta machine set to a medium-thick setting. Place the clay cane on the gold sheet, lining up one end of the cane with one edge of the sheet. Use a tissue blade to trim any excess gold sheet that extends beyond the opposite end of the cane.
7 Roll up the cane in one layer of the clay sheet. Use a craft knife to trim excess sheet. Smooth the seam with your fingers or a smoothing tool.

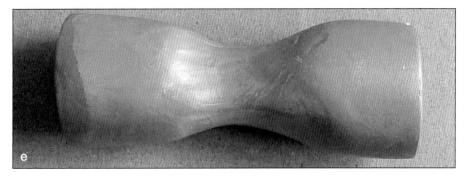

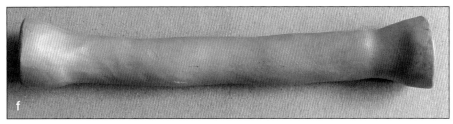

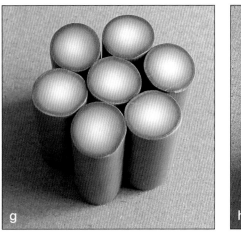

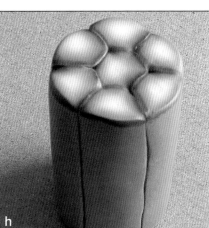

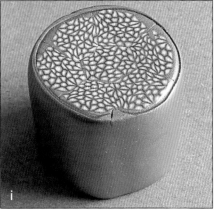

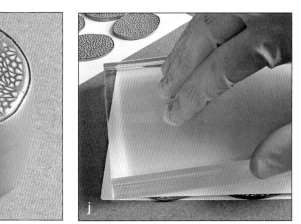

8 To reduce the cane, hold it in one hand and gently squeeze its middle, creating an hourglass shape (photo e). Working from the center to the ends, continue to squeeze the remainder of the cane to reduce its diameter (photo f). Continue to gently squeeze, pull, and smooth the cane until it lengthens to 11½ in. (29.2cm).

9 Using your palms, roll the cane on your work surface to even out its shape and to remove the indentations made by squeezing it. Use a tissue blade to trim ½ in. (1.3cm) from each end of the cane.

10 Using a tissue blade, cut the cane into seven equal-length pieces. Build a large cane by grouping six pieces around the seventh, as shown (photo g). Even out the edges of the large cane by gently rolling it on your work surface (photo h).

11 Reduce the cane as you did previously; gently squeeze its middle, then move toward each end, pulling and smoothing the cane until it's 11½ in. long. Roll the cane on your work surface to even out its shape. Trim the ends, and cut it into seven equal-length pieces.

12 Build another large cane by grouping six of the pieces around the seventh. Roll the cane to smooth its edges. Then repeat the steps to reduce, roll, trim, cut, build, and roll the cane one last time. The cane should be approximately 1¼ in. (3.2cm) long and 1¼ in. in diameter.

TIP: If the cane's diameter is too small, gently press the ends toward one another. This adds girth to the cane and shortens its length.

13 Set the pasta machine to thin and run a sheet of gold clay through it. Wrap this sheet around the cane the

DESIGNER'S NOTE: The polymer clay formulations that work best for cane making are the stiffer clays, such as Fimo Classic and Kato Polyclay. Cane making is about building patterns that have distinct color separations that remain crisp after the pattern is reduced. Stiffer clays hold up to this challenge. Softer clay formulations tend to yield canes with patterns that get blurry because the components in the cane mush together as you reduce the cane.

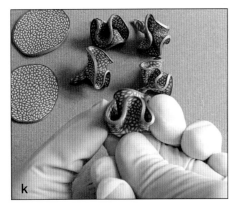

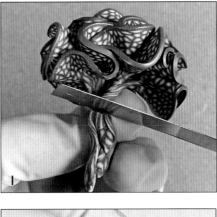

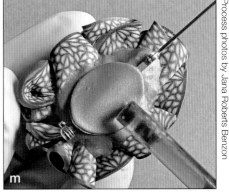

Process photos by Jana Roberts Benzon

same way you wrapped the color-blend cane (photo i).

14 Put on a dust mask and use a soft-tip paintbrush to apply a light layer of mica powder to the outside of the cane.

15 Set the cane aside to rest for 30 minutes. This allows the cane to cool a little, which makes it easier to cut. However, don't let the cane rest for longer than 30 minutes, or it will become too stiff to manipulate without cracking.

16 Use a tissue blade to trim the cane's ragged ends. (When you're cutting cane slices, you'll get better results if your tissue blade is sharp and free of nicks.) Then cut six or seven ¹/₁₆-in. (2mm)-thick slices.

17 Lay the slices on an index card and place another index card on top of them. Use an acrylic block to gently rub the surface of the top card to make the slices a consistent thickness (photo j).

18 Pick up a cane slice and pinch its center gently between your thumb and forefinger. Using your other hand, make a series of loose folds in the edges of the cane slice (photo k). Be sure to leave crevices between the folds that are wide enough to cradle any beads or small items you want to insert later. Repeat to softly fold the remaining cane slices.

19 As if you were making a bouquet, hold a component by its pinch point in one hand, and then add a second component, compressing the pinch points together. Continue to add components until you're satisfied with the size and shape of the cluster. This process creates a clay stem that extends from the center of the cluster's back.

20 Use a tissue blade to carefully cut off the clay stem at the base of the cluster (photo l).

21 Place the cluster right side up on a ceramic tile, and bake it according to the clay manufacturer's instructions. Allow the cluster to cool.

22 Make a ¹/₁₆-in. (1.5mm)-thick disk of gold clay that's the same length as your pin-back finding and about ³/₈ in. (1cm) wide. Use a fine-tip paintbrush to apply a coat of liquid polymer clay to one side of the disk. Press the coated side of the disk against the center back of the cured cluster. Use a smoothing tool to smooth and press the disk into the crevices on the bottom of the cluster.

23 Open the pin back and gently press it into the surface of the disk.

24 Make a second ¹/₁₆-in. (1.5mm)-thick disk of gold clay that is large enough to cover the length of your pin back without covering the pin catch or hinge.

25 Apply a coat of liquid polymer clay to one side of the disk and place it coated-side down over the pin back. Use a smoothing tool to lightly press the top disk to the bottom disk, sandwiching the pin back between the two layers of clay (photo m).

26 I like to make an assembly to support my brooch during the baking cycle. I cut a pin-back-sized slot in a cardboard box, insert the pin back

(photo n), and then bake the brooch (box and all). (Make sure that the box and brooch do not touch the heating elements in your oven.) Bake according to the clay manufacturer's instructions.

27 After the brooch is cool, use tweezers to place stone beads, shells, glass beads, or other items in the crevices of the folds (photo o). If you're using drilled beads, position them so that the holes are concealed.

28 In a well-ventilated area, mix two-part epoxy according to the clay manufacturer's instructions. Use a toothpick to apply the epoxy to the areas of the beads that come in contact with the inner folds of the clay. Allow the epoxy to cure completely.

CANING

Beadrock

Rockin' polymer clay beads
mimic chunky stone nuggets in
a substantial but lightweight
necklace with prehistoric appeal

designed by **Lori Wilkes**

supplies:

**13 nugget beads, each ¾–1½ in.
(1.9–3.8cm)**

- 2 oz. polymer clay in each of
  6–8 colors
- acrylic paint
- aluminum foil
- bead curing tray (optional)
- cornstarch
- flexible stamp
- acrylic floor finish
- needle tool or piercing needles
- paintbrush
- paper towel
- pasta machine*
- 4-in. (10cm) acrylic rolling sheet
- tissue blade
- toaster oven*
- nonstick work surface

*Dedicated to use with polymer clay

necklace, 16 in. (41cm)

- 14 6mm fire-polished beads
- 4 4mm fire-polished beads
  (optional)
- clasp
- 2 crimp beads
- flexible beading wire, .019
- crimping pliers
- wire cutters

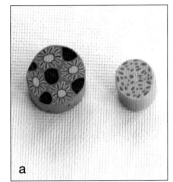

a

b

c

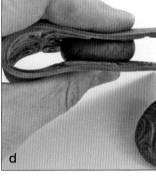

d

e

f

g

h

Millefiori canes

To begin this project, make two different millefiori canes in your chosen color schemes (photo a). For ideas, see the other caning projets in this section.

Millefiori beads

1 Roll a ball of scrap clay that is approximately 1½ x ¾ in. (3.8 x 1.9cm). Make eight more balls in pairs of gradually smaller sizes.

2 With the tissue blade, cut thin slices from the millefiori canes. Apply the slices to cover the scrap clay balls (photo b), making pairs that match in pattern and size.

3 Roll each ball with the acrylic square until the edges of the cane slices blend together and the seams disappear. Gently press the balls until they are pebble shaped (photo c).

4 Using a needle tool, make a hole through each pebble-shaped ball.

Textured beads

1 Condition and mix clay to the desired color (I used copper and gold), and roll four balls that are similar in size to the millefiori beads.

2 Dust the flexible stamp with cornstarch. This will allow the stamp to release from the clay easily.

3 Sandwich a clay ball between the folded stamp, and gently press to slightly flatten the clay (photo d). Check if the impression is deep enough. If not, roll the clay again, and repeat.

4 Repeat steps 2 and 3 with the remaining balls.

5 Use a needle tool or piercing needle to make a hole through each stamped and flattened ball (needles can be left in the beads for baking).

Baking and finishing

1 Place the clay beads onto a bead curing tray (photo e). Shield the beads with an aluminum foil tent to keep them from scorching. Following the clay manufacturer's instructions, bake the beads in the toaster oven. Allow the beads to cool completely.

2 Paint the textured beads with acrylic paint (photo f). To simulate a copper patina, I used green paint. Use a dampened paper towel to remove most of the paint, leaving the paint in the recessed areas (photo g).

3 Use a paintbrush to apply acrylic floor finish to the millefiori beads (photo h). Allow them to dry.

Necklace assembly

1 Cut 22 in. (56cm) of beading wire, and center the largest millefiori bead on it. On each wire

end, string a repeating pattern of a 6mm fire-polished bead and a polymer bead, stringing the polymer beads from largest to smallest. End with a 6mm.

2 Test the fit, and add or remove beads if necessary. I added two 4mm fire-polished beads at each end.

3 On each end, string a crimp bead and half of the clasp. Go back through the crimp and the last few beads. Crimp the crimp beads, and trim the excess wire.

CANING

Craft a seamless cuff

Learn expert techniques to bond cane veneers to an aluminum blank

designed by **Melanie West**

supplies:
cuff, 13/16 x 2¾ in. (2.1 x 7cm)
- polymer clay
  - 4 oz. black
  - 2 oz. white
- white craft glue
- 1 x 6 in. (2.5 x 15cm) 20-gauge shaped aluminum cuff blank
- tissue blade
- craft knife
- needle tool
- smoothing tool
- acrylic roller
- soft cloth
- pasta machine*
- toaster oven*
- polyester fiberfill
- sandpaper, various grits
- buffing machine
- nonstick work surface

*Dedicated to use with polymer clay

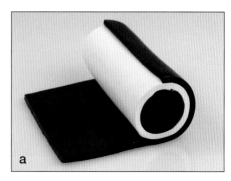

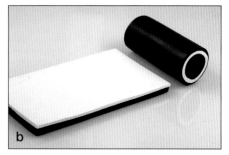

The best way I've found to make a polymer clay cuff is to use an aluminum blank as an armature. Aluminum is lightweight, flexible but sturdy, and economical. You can buy aluminum cuff blanks or make your own.

Striped bull's-eye cane

The black-and-white bull's-eye striped cane is a basic pattern that lends itself to interpretation; for example, you could try using different colors or varying the width of the stripes. As a general rule, remember that if you want a graphic, well-defined design, you must place a light color between two dark colors and vice versa.

1 Separately condition black and white polymer clays.

2 Using the black clay, make a cylinder approximately 1 in. (2.5cm) in diameter and at least 2 in. (5cm) long.

3 Run the white clay through the pasta machine set to the thickest setting. Use a tissue blade to cut the white sheet into a rectangle, making the short sides the same length as the black clay cylinder.

4 Wrap the white rectangle around the cylinder, and use a craft knife to trim the excess white clay. Use a smoothing tool to blend the seam. Use this technique whenever you add a layer to the cane.

5 Run black clay through the pasta machine set to the thickest setting, and cut it into a rectangle, as you did with the white clay. Add this layer to the cane to make a bull's-eye cane (photo a).

6 To make a striped cane, run more black and white clay separately through the pasta machine at its thickest setting. Use the craft knife to cut each clay sheet into rectangles that have short sides that are equal to the length of the bull's-eye cane and long sides that are twice as long as the short sides.

7 Stack a white rectangle on top of a black rectangle (photo b). To prevent air bubbles from getting trapped between the layers of clay, use an acrylic roller to roll from the center to one end of the stack. Repeat to roll from the center to the opposite end.

8 Stack and roll two more rectangles, alternating colors. The stack should now be four layers thick. Use a tissue blade to cut the stack in half along its width to create two stacks of four layers each.

9 Place one stack on top of the other, maintaining the striped pattern, to make a cane that's eight layers thick. When placed short end up, the striped cane should be as tall as your bull's-eye cane (photo c).

EDITOR'S NOTE:
For this project, use a brand of clay that's both durable and flexible after curing to provide the right amount of give for a cuff bracelet, such as Kato Polyclay.

CANING

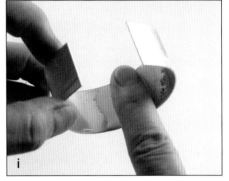

10 Allow the cane to rest. Set the striped cane aside to cool and rest for approximately 30 minutes.

TIP: Cool clay is stiffer than warm clay. Cool clay is easier to cut into slices without distorting a pattern.

11 Use your tissue blade to impress vertical cutting guidelines into the short end of the striped cane, keeping the lines equally spaced and perpendicular to the striped pattern **(photo d)**.

NOTE: You'll need to cut enough slices from the striped cane so they can wrap around the bull's-eye cane when attached with long sides together.

12 Following your scored guidelines, use the tissue blade to cut the striped cane into slices.

TIP: Always use a tissue blade that is clean, sharp, and free of nicks to cut cane slices. This keeps the cane from distorting and the colors from mushing.

13 Arrange the slices so their long sides butt against each other to create a striped sheet. Level the surface of the sheet by using your tissue blade to remove any excess clay **(photo e)**.

14 Gently run your acrylic roller over the striped sheet to help the edges of the slices stick together. Don't use so much pressure that you begin to distort the striped pattern.

15 Carefully add the striped sheet to the bull's-eye cane **(photo f)**. If the stripes separate, gently press them together, without distorting the pattern.

16 Run white clay through the pasta machine on its thickest setting. Cut this sheet into a rectangle and add this layer to the cane **(photo g)**.

17 Run black clay through the pasta machine on a medium-thick setting. Cut the sheet into a rectangle and add the layer to the cane. Repeat to add another layer **(photo h)**.

NOTE: The number of black clay layers you add to your cane will determine the distance between the circle patterns on your finished cuff. The more layers of black clay you add, the thicker the black border between the circle patterns.

18 To reduce the cane, gently squeeze the cane at its middle, creating an hour-glass shape. Working from the center to the ends, continue to squeeze the remainder of the cane to reduce its diameter. Continue to reduce the cane to

your desired size. I reduced mine to about ⅜ in. (1cm) in diameter.

19 Set the cane aside to rest for about 30 minutes.

Cane-slice veneer

1 While your cane is resting, apply a thin coat of white craft glue to the top and underside of an aluminum cuff blank **(photo i)**. Allow the glue to dry completely.

2 Use a clean, sharp tissue blade to cut ⅛-in. (3mm)-thick slices from your cane **(photo j)**.

3 Lay the slices on the surface of the blank so that they fit together without gaps. You might have to gently shape the outside edges of some of the slices to achieve a good fit **(photo k)**. Reshape the edges only slightly to minimize the distortion of the cane pattern.

4 Continue to add slices, allowing the slices along the edge of the blank to extend a bit beyond the metal surface, until you've covered about 2 in. (5cm) of the blank.

5 Following the edge of the blank as a guide, use an old tissue blade to trim the excess clay **(photo l)**. (A new tissue blade is quickly dulled by the aluminum blank.)

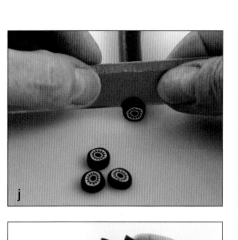

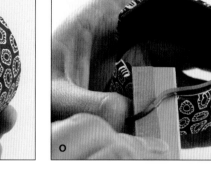

TIP: Dull tissue blades, as well as sharp ones, should be used with great care. The safest way to use a blade is to cut away from yourself. (**Photo k** shows the opposite only to give you a better view.)

6 Continue to add slices and trim excess clay until you've completely covered the front of the blank.

7 Because the cuff will be assembled and baked several times, you need to safeguard against overheating the clay. The polyester fiberfill will help. Place two layers of polyester fiberfill on a baking tray and place the blank assembly on the fiberfill. Place two more layers of fiberfill over the assembly, and cover the entire baking tray with aluminum foil. Bake the assembly according to the clay manufacturer's instructions. Allow the assembly to air-cool completely.

8 Put on a dust mask and use 320-grit sandpaper to lightly dry-sand the edges of the clay.

NOTE: Do not wet-sand the clay; water could get into any gaps between the blank and the clay, which could wash away the glue or cause the clay to crack.

9 Add a sheet of clay to the underside of the armature: Run black clay through

the pasta machine on a medium-thick setting to make a sheet at least 6½ in. (16.5cm) long. From the sheet, cut a strip of clay that's slightly longer and wider than the blank. Lay the strip of clay against the underside of the blank (**photo m**).

10 Starting at the middle of the clay strip and working toward the ends, gently roll your finger against the clay to secure it to the blank and to force out any air that could be trapped between the blank and the clay (**photo n**).

NOTE: Air that gets trapped between the blank and the clay will create air bubbles, which appear as bumps on the surface of the clay. To release trapped air, use a needle tool to pierce any bumps and then use a smoothing tool to close the hole.

11 Use your old tissue blade to trim the excess clay flush with the edge of the blank (**photo o**).

12 Prepare the assembly as you did previously, protecting it with fiberfill and foil. Bake again and allow the assembly to air-cool completely.
13 Using your finger, apply a thin coat of liquid polymer clay along the edges of the assembly (photo p). Use a paper towel to wipe away any liquid clay that gets on the top or underside of the assembly.

TIP: Remove sticky liquid polymer clay from your hands using a paper towel moistened with rubbing alcohol.

14 Run black clay through the pasta machine on its thickest setting. Cut several strips from this sheet, making sure that they're a bit wider than the depth of the assembly.
15 Lay one strip along the edge of the cuff, keeping one edge of the strip flush with the clay covering the underside of the blank (photo q).
16 Use your fingers to gently blend the edge of the strip into the cured clay on the underside of the blank (photo r). Don't worry about blending it perfectly; you'll sand it smooth later. Continue adding strips and blending their edges into the cured clay until all the edges of the cuff are covered.

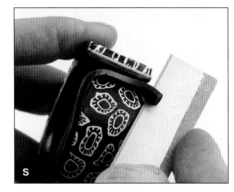

17 Using the outer, cured clay edge as a guide for your tissue blade, trim the excess clay (photo s).
18 After you have trimmed all the excess clay, check for any gaps between the top cured layer of clay and the raw clay strip. If you find any gaps, use gentle pressure to bond the raw clay to the cured clay (photo t).
19 Protect, bake the cuff again, and allow the bracelet to air-cool completely.

Finishing

1 Fill a bowl with water and a few drops of dishwashing soap. The soap will help keep the wet/dry sandpaper from becoming clogged as you sand the cuff. Keep the cuff and sandpaper wet during the sanding process.

TIP: Changing the water each time you switch to the next finer grit of sandpaper will help minimize clogging.

2 For a satin finish, sand all the surfaces of the cuff with 320-grit sandpaper. Progress to 400- and 600 grit. Then, rub the cuff with a clean, soft cotton cloth. For a lacquer-like finish, sand the surfaces with 320-, 400-, 600-, 1000-, 1200-, 1500-, and finally 2000-grit sandpaper. Use a buffing machine to give the cuff a high shine if desired.

EDITOR'S NOTES:
Creating a veneer with cane slices is just one way to cover the top of your cuff. Other options include using a clay sheet that you've customized with surface treatments such as: silk-screened patterns, ink-stamped designs, alcohol ink painting or washes, or mica powder effects.

Apply a coat of translucent liquid polymer clay prior to baking. Use a gentle touch when sanding to avoid removing the surface treatments.

Colorfusion

Piece together a polymer clay puzzle with fresh colors and funky shapes

designed by **Kim Otterbein**

You'll need:

polymer clay tube, 7½ in. (19.1cm) with 2-in. (5cm) teardrop dangle

- polymer clay: navy blue, pink, dark red, white, ochre, light blue; 2–4 oz. each
- 71 in. (1.8m) 18-gauge half-hard sterling silver wire
- 3 in. (7.6cm) 16-gauge half-hard square sterling silver wire
- **48** 5mm inside diameter 18-gauge sterling silver jump rings

- nonstick work surface
- pasta machine*
- tissue blade
- acrylic rolling sheet
- flatnose pliers
- roundnose pliers
- wire cutters
- toaster oven*
- superglue
- wet/dry sandpaper (optional)
- hammer
- steel bench block

*Dedicated to use with polymer clay

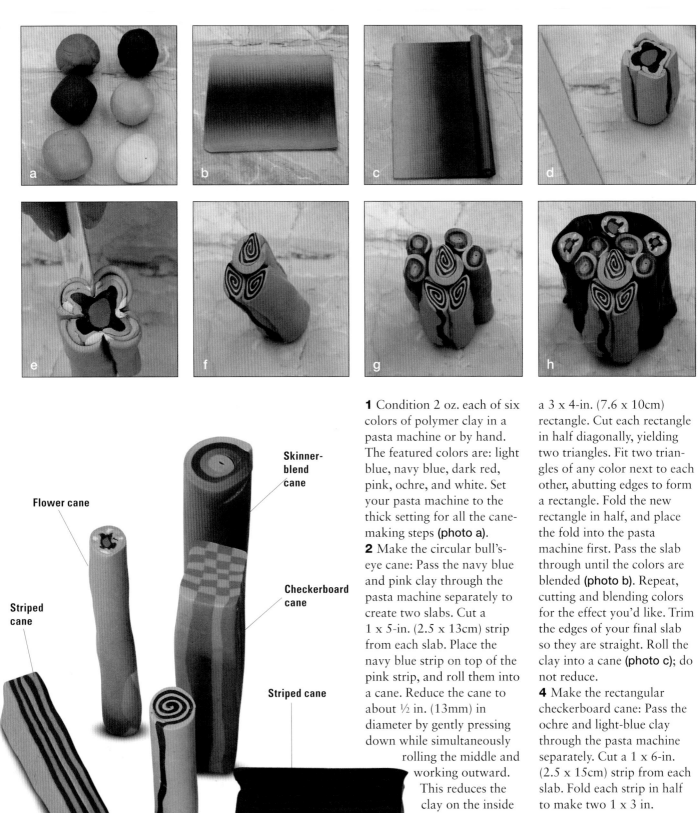

a

b

c

d

e

f

g

h

Flower cane

Skinner-blend cane

Striped cane

Checkerboard cane

Striped cane

Bull's-eye cane

1 Condition 2 oz. each of six colors of polymer clay in a pasta machine or by hand. The featured colors are: light blue, navy blue, dark red, pink, ochre, and white. Set your pasta machine to the thick setting for all the cane-making steps (photo a).

2 Make the circular bull's-eye cane: Pass the navy blue and pink clay through the pasta machine separately to create two slabs. Cut a 1 x 5-in. (2.5 x 13cm) strip from each slab. Place the navy blue strip on top of the pink strip, and roll them into a cane. Reduce the cane to about ½ in. (13mm) in diameter by gently pressing down while simultaneously rolling the middle and working outward. This reduces the clay on the inside at the same rate as the clay on the outside.

3 Make the circular Skinner-blend cane: Pass the red, ochre, and pink clay through the pasta machine separately. Cut each slab into

a 3 x 4-in. (7.6 x 10cm) rectangle. Cut each rectangle in half diagonally, yielding two triangles. Fit two triangles of any color next to each other, abutting edges to form a rectangle. Fold the new rectangle in half, and place the fold into the pasta machine first. Pass the slab through until the colors are blended (photo b). Repeat, cutting and blending colors for the effect you'd like. Trim the edges of your final slab so they are straight. Roll the clay into a cane (photo c); do not reduce.

4 Make the rectangular checkerboard cane: Pass the ochre and light-blue clay through the pasta machine separately. Cut a 1 x 6-in. (2.5 x 15cm) strip from each slab. Fold each strip in half to make two 1 x 3 in. (2.5 x 7.6cm) strips.

5 Put the ochre strip on top of the light blue strip. Cut the stack in half, and place the light-blue side on top of the ochre side. Repeat once more so the finished stack is light

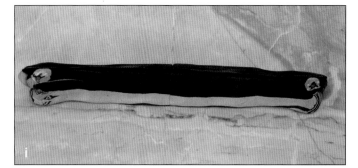

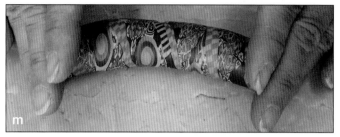

blue on the bottom and ochre on the top.

6 Cut the stack lengthwise into equal strips. Looking at the end of the stack, flip every other strip to make a checkerboard pattern. Reduce to ½ x 3 in. (1.3 x 7.6cm), keeping the cane rectangular.

7 Make two rectangular striped canes: Pass the navy blue and red clay through the pasta machine separately. Cut a 1 x 6-in. (2.5 x 15cm) strip from each slab. Cut each strip in half lengthwise. Put a navy blue strip on top of a red strip. Repeat, cutting strips and alternating colors, until the stack is ½ in. (1.3cm) thick. Reduce the cane to ½ x 3 in. (1.3 x 7.6cm). Make another striped cane in a different color combination.

8 To make the circular flower cane, make a ¼ x 1-in. (6 x 25mm) snake in light blue. Pass a small amount of navy blue through the pasta machine, and wrap the navy blue slab around the light-blue snake.

9 Make four 1-in. (25.5mm) red snakes, and position

them around the outside of the navy blue core.

10 Pass the pink clay through the pasta machine. Cut the slab into eight equal strips. Fit a pink strip around the outside of each red snake. Fit the remaining four pink strips around the first four pink strips **(photo d)**. Make four 1-in. (25.5mm) white snakes, and position them in the gaps between the pink strips.

11 Make a ½ x 1-in. (13 x 25.5mm) slab of ochre, and wrap it around the whole cane. Press a credit card into four sides of the cane, making petals **(photo e)**. Reduce the cane to about ½ in. (13mm) in diameter.

12 Make the main cane: Cut the bull's-eye cane into three 1½-in. (38mm), horizontal sections. Save the rest. Pinch lengthwise along the sides of each section, making the sections elliptical. Group these sections with a strip of ochre between them **(photo f)**.

13 Cut the Skinner-blend cane in half horizontally, and reduce one of the halves to about ⅜ in. (1cm). Cut the reduced half into four equal sections. Add these sections

to the bull's-eye sections **(photo g)**. Make a thin slab of navy blue, and wrap it around the Skinner-blend sections.

14 Cut the flower cane into three horizontal sections, and add them to the outside of the navy blue slab. Cut a ¼-in. (6mm) section from one of the striped canes, and cut that section in half. Add the sections to the outside. Make another thin slab of navy blue, and wrap it around the outside **(photo h)**.

15 Press this grouping into a triangle **(photo i)**, and carefully reduce it, maintaining the shape as you simultaneously pull the sides and gently press down to lengthen it. Reduce the cane to about 6 in. (15cm) long.

16 Cut the triangle in half horizontally, and group the two triangle sections vertically **(photo j)**. Gently press the sections together. Reduce the cane again to 6 in. long, maintaining a wide triangular shape.

17 Cut the triangle in half horizontally, and group the halves vertically to make a square cane **(photo k)**.

Reduce the cane to about 8 in. (20cm) long.

18 Roll the core of the necklace tube: Use spare clay to roll a ½ x 7-in. (1.3 x 18cm) snake in any color or combination of colors. You'll be trimming about 1¼ in. (3.2cm) from the ends, so keep that in mind as you determine the length.

19 Cut very thin slices from all the canes, and arrange them on the core without overlapping. Gently press them into place. Cut slices creatively to fill spaces. You can also reduce a cane further to fit slices into smaller spaces, but maintain variety by cutting the cane in half, reducing one half, and leaving the other half its original size.

20 When the core is completely covered **(photo l)**, gently shorten and fatten the necklace tube by rolling from the outside edges to the inside, using very light pressure to push the clay toward the middle **(photo m)**.

21 Use an acrylic rolling sheet to even out the shape, smooth the seams, and lengthen the tube to about 7 in. **(photo n)**. Cut a ¾-in.

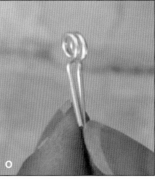

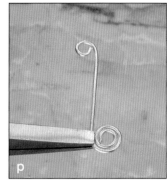

(1.9cm) piece from one end for use in making the dangle in the next step. Trim the other end as necessary to even it out. Cap each end of the tube with a cane slice if desired.

22 Wrap the leftover canes in plastic to use for another project. They'll keep indefinitely.

23 Shape the ¾-in. piece of tube into an elongated teardrop.

24 Cut three 2-in. (5cm) pieces of 18-gauge wire.

25 Wrap the center of one piece of wire twice around one jaw of your roundnose pliers. Bring both wire ends together, facing the same direction. Cut the wire tails to about ⅜ in. long **(photo o)**. Repeat to make a second finding. Press one wire finding into each end of the necklace tube.

26 Make a third finding for the dangle, but leave only one wire tail; the dangle is too thin at the top to accommodate both tails. Press this wire finding into the dangle.

27 Bend the necklace tube into a loose U shape. To see how it will look, gently pick it up and hold it in front of a mirror. Place the shaped tube and the dangles on a piece of cardboard and bake according to the clay manufacturer's instructions. Let the pieces cool in the oven.

28 After the pieces are cool, pull out the findings, put a drop of glue on each, and place them back into the clay pieces.

29 Because the necklace tube was rolled with plastic, it should be very smooth. If it needs additional sanding, start with 600-grit sandpaper, and progress to finer grits. The design is only a thin layer, so be careful not to sand too much.

30 Cut 11 2¾-in. (7cm) pieces of 18-gauge wire. This will make a 7-in. (18cm) chain and a necklace length of 23 in. (58cm).

31 To make a chain component, use roundnose pliers to form a small circle at the end of one wire. The circle should be large enough to hold two jump rings. Using flatnose pliers, grasp the circle horizontally. Form the wire tail around the circle with your fingers to create a coil **(photo p)**. Coil the tail to the middle of the wire only. Repeat on the other end of the wire, coiling in the opposite direction. Make 11 chain components. Flatten the components with a hammer on a steel bench block to work-harden them.

32 Cut a 3-in. piece of 16-gauge square wire. Hammer one end to slightly flatten it. Using roundnose pliers, curl the flat end of the wire into a small circle. Lightly hammer the other end of the wire. Using the tip of your roundnose pliers, make a tight little curl in the same direction as the first. Grasp the center of the wire with the thickest part of your roundnose pliers, and fold the wire over to form a hook. Hammer the loop of the hook.

33 Use jump rings to attach a chain component to one side of the necklace tube. Use jump rings to link half of the remaining chain components on one side of the necklace. Repeat on the other side of the necklace. Use jump rings to attach the teardrop dangle to one end of the chain and the hook to the other **(photo q)**.

supplies:

**pendant, 1⅜ x 2½ in.
(3.5 x 6.4cm)**

- polymer clay
  - 4 oz. light gold
  - 3 oz. brown
  - 1 oz. rose
  - 1½ oz. gold
  - 4½ oz. cream
  - 3 oz. black
- liquid polymer clay
- 24 in. (61cm) 2mm
  rubber cord
- **2** beads with 2mm holes
- tissue blade
- acrylic roller
- pasta machine*
- nonstick work surface
- tissue blade
- needle tool
- ripple blade
- rounded tool (optional)
- latex gloves (optional)
- knitting needle or
  smoothing tool
- nonstick work surface
- toaster oven*
- wet/dry sandpaper (800-,
  1000-, 1200-, 1500-,
  2000-grit); 2500-grit
  (optional)
- fine-tip paintbrush
- cornstarch
- upholstery needle
- buffing machine (optional)
- flex shaft or rotary tool, bit
  to fit two thicknesses of
  rubber cord
- superglue

*Dedicated to use with
polymer clay

Note: If using a premade
cane, choose a rectangular
or square, millefiori or other
pattern, 1¼-in. (3.2cm)
diameter, ½-in. (1.3cm)
long cane

Millefiori masterpiece

Shape a complex cane into a sleek pendant and slide closure

designed by **Jana Roberts Benzon**

With a little patience and wet/ dry sandpaper in successively finer grits, you can give polymer clay a soft sheen. The extra step of buffing brings the surface to a glass-like luster. Add color and depth to a pendant and necklace slide with your own cane, or purchase a cane from a supplier.

Making the cane

1 Separately condition each color of clay until it is soft and pliable.

2 Make a Skinner blend using 1 oz. of rose polymer clay and 1 oz. of light gold polymer clay. Beginning at the light-colored end, roll the blend into a cylinder.

3 Run black clay through the pasta machine at a medium setting. Wrap the sheet of black clay around the cylinder.

4 Reduce and lengthen the cylinder by squeezing it in the center and working out toward each end until you have a 5-in. (13cm) snake. Roll the snake to a uniform diameter, and then gently pull it to 11 in. (28cm). Roll the snake again to remove any lumps. Trim the ragged ends, leaving a 10-in. (25cm) snake.

5 Use a tissue blade to cut the snake into five 2-in. (5cm) segments. Pinch along the length of each segment, creating a teardrop shape for the petals.

6 To create the center of the flower, roll a ball of gold clay until it is 2 in. (51mm) long and thick enough that the wide ends of the petals fit snugly around it. Place the petals around the center. Fill the spaces between the petals with triangular wedges of cream clay as shown **(photo a)**, making sure there are no gaps. Maintaining

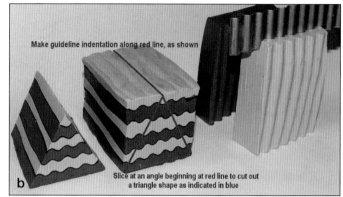

Make guideline indentation along red line, as shown

Slice at an angle beginning at red line to cut out a triangle shape as indicated in blue

the roundness of the flower component, smooth the edges of the clay, and squeeze gently to fuse the pieces. Use a needle tool to mark a line along the length of one petal. Pinch along the line to form the flower component into a teardrop shape.

7 Run black clay through the pasta machine at a medium-thin setting. Wrap the black sheet around the flower component. Carefully trim the ragged ends, and set aside.

8 Make layered, rippled triangles: Form the cream clay into a rectangular block that's 2½ in. (6.4cm) long, 3 in. (7.6cm) wide, and 1¾ in. (4.4cm) high. Repeat with the brown clay to make a second block. Set the blocks aside, or refrigerate them until the clay is stiff.

9 Set each block on its 1¾ x 3-in. end. Use a ripple blade to take several ¼-in. (6mm) slices from each block. Cut slowly, keeping the blade straight and maintaining even cuts.

10 Run black clay through the pasta machine at a thin setting. Place a slice of rippled brown clay on your work surface. Lay the black sheet on top, and use a rounded tool to press the layers together. Next, layer a slice of rippled cream clay. Then, layer another sheet of thin black clay. Repeat this pattern, using a rounded tool

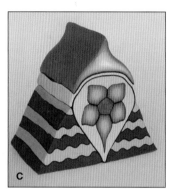

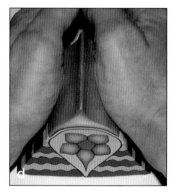

between each layer, until the block has three brown layers and three cream layers. Repeat the sequence to make a second rippled block.

11 Trim the ragged edges, and use an acrylic roller to smooth the bottom of each block. Following the grain of the ripple, use a needle tool to mark a line along the center on the top of each block. Cut a triangular wedge from each block, using the line you just made to guide your tissue blade **(photo b)**.

12 Make a Skinner blend using 1 oz. of gold clay and 1 oz. of cream clay. Starting at the light-colored end, roll the blend into a cylinder. Reduce the cylinder to ¾ in. (1.9cm) in diameter.

13 Cut a 2-in. (5cm) segment from the cylinder. Form the segment into a triangle by pinching three evenly spaced points along its entire length. Keeping the three edges crisp, use your fingers to shape an

arch between two of the pinched points.

14 Place the arch on top of the rounded end of the flower component, adjusting the curve of the arch as necessary for a snug fit but without allowing the two pieces to fuse. Separate the triangle from the flower component.

15 Run black clay through the pasta machine at a medium-thin setting, and then place it only on the arch of the triangle.

16 Set the rippled triangles on your work surface so that they nearly touch. Place the point of the flower component into the crevice between the two triangles, and then gently compress and fuse the flower and triangles.

17 Run cream clay through the pasta machine at a medium-thick setting. Cut it to lay over the rounded top of the flower component, and then center the triangle on top of it **(photo c)**. With the palms of your hands, firmly press the sides of the triangle to flatten and even up the sides **(photo d)**. Sharpen the edges of the cane and use your thumbs and forefingers to smooth the lumps. Use a tissue blade to trim just enough from each end of the cane to yield a smooth surface **(photo e)**.

18 Allow the cane to rest for at least six hours before reducing it. After the resting period, you will need to "wake up" the inside of the cane so that it will reduce properly. Warm up the cane by slamming each side on a stable work surface. When the ends of the cane begin to bulge, the center is warm, and the cane will begin to reduce. Continue to slam the cane, alternating sides, until it becomes too lengthy to easily manage.

19 Then, press on the sides with the heels of your hands, starting at the center and squeezing toward the ends. Turn the cane over, and

continue to squeeze from the center to the ends, turning the cane so that each side receives an equal amount of pressure. Run your thumb and forefinger along the edges to keep them crisp. If the edges are not reducing as much as the sides, lengthen the edges by gently pulling them.

20 To continue reducing the cane, stroke your hands along its length, rotating the cane between strokes. When the cane is about 10 in. (25cm) long, further reduce it by holding each end while you very gently pull and tap it on your work surface. Continue to reduce and smooth it until each side of the triangle is about ¾ in. (1.9cm). Trim the ragged ends.

21 Cut the cane into six equal pieces. Arrange the six pieces into a hexagon by placing the gold triangles in the center and then matching up the lines **(photo f)**.

22 To shape the cane into a rectangle for the pendant, use gentle pressure to simultaneously press two opposing points on the outside of the cane **(photo g)**. To make a round cane, press two opposing points as you would for a rectangle, but then continue to rotate and press two more points. Repeat until the cane is round.

Making the pendant

1 Condition 2 oz. of black clay. Wear latex gloves to avoid leaving fingerprints on the clay. A smooth surface is easier to sand, so it's easier to obtain a shiny finish. Shape the conditioned black clay into a half-cylinder that is 1⅜ in. (3.5cm) long, ⅞ in. (2.2cm) wide, and ⅜ in. (1cm) high **(photo h)**. Use a knitting needle or smoothing tool to smooth the surface of the pendant base.

2 Place the pendant base on a ceramic tile, and bake it according to the clay

manufacturer's instructions. Allow the pendant base to cool completely.

3 Fill a bowl with tepid water, and dip the pendant base and 800-grit wet/dry sandpaper in the water. Sand the surface of the pendant base, making eight to ten swipes. Repeat, using wet/dry sandpapers in progressively finer grits. A 1000-, 1200-, 1500-, and 2000-grit sandpaper progression gives the polymer a high shine. For best results, frequently replenish the bowl with fresh water.

4 Select or make a rectangular millefiori cane that is at least 1¼-in. (3.2cm) wide and 1 in. (2.5cm) high.

5 Use a tissue blade to cut two ¹⁄₁₆-in. (1.5mm) slices from the cane. Set them aside to use in the necklace slide.

6 Wrap the cane in black clay. Run black clay through the pasta machine on a very thin setting, or roll the clay to 1mm thick. Wrap this sheet around the cane. Chill the cane in the refrigerator to make it easier to slice without distorting it.

7 Attach a cane slice to the pendant base. Cut a ⅛-in. (3mm) slice from the cane. Place the slice on the pendant base, leaving ⅛ in. of the pendant base visible on the left and right sides. Smooth and shape the slice to match the contour of the pendant base. Gently remove the slice, and use a paintbrush to apply a small amount of liquid clay to the back of the slice. Return the slice to the base, and smooth the surface.

8 Make a tube bail: Roll black clay into a 1-in. (2.5cm) snake with a ¼-in. (6.5mm) diameter. Apply cornstarch to an upholstery needle, and insert the needle halfway through one end of

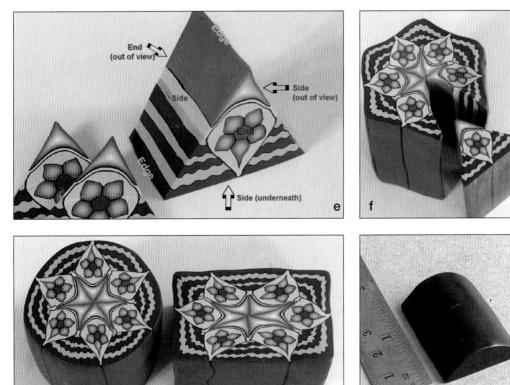

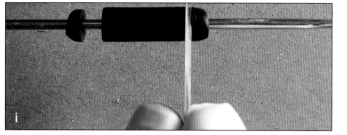

Process photos by Jana Roberts Benzon

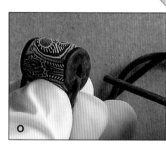

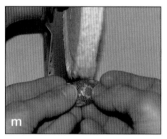

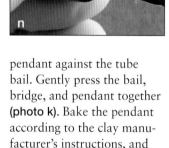

the snake. Remove the needle and insert it into the opposite end. Gently push the needle all the way through the snake. Rotate the needle to form a hole that is large enough to fit the rubber cord. With the needle still in the tube, gently roll the tube on your work surface to smooth the clay. Trim any ragged ends (photo i).

9 Make a clay bridge: Run a small amount of black clay through the pasta machine at a medium-thick setting, or roll it out to 1/16 in. (1.5mm) thick. Cut a 1/2 x 1/2-in. (13 x 13mm) square from this sheet.

10 Attach the tube bail to the pendant. Coat one side of the clay bridge with liquid clay. Center the tube bail on the top edge of the bridge (photo j). Dab liquid clay on the pendant where you will position the bridge. Attach the pendant to the bridge, abutting the top of the

pendant against the tube bail. Gently press the bail, bridge, and pendant together (photo k). Bake the pendant according to the clay manufacturer's instructions, and allow it to cool.

11 To make the necklace slide, roll black clay into a 1/2-in. (1.3cm) tube with a 3/8-in. (1cm) diameter. Place the cane slices you set aside earlier around the tube, and trim any excess clay. Smooth the seam. Make two pea-sized balls of black clay. Flatten the balls, place one at each end of the tube, and smooth the seams (photo l). Bake the slide and allow it to cool

12 Sand the pendant and slide using the same sanding progression that you used to sand the pendant base. For additional shine, use brief, light pressure to buff the pendant and slide with an electric buffer fitted

with a stitched muslin buff (photo m).

13 Mark the center point of each end of the slide. Use a flex shaft or rotary tool with a drill bit that will make a hole just large enough to accept two passes of the rubber cord, and drill halfway through the slide. Turn the slide over, and drill through the other half. Move the drill bit back and forth to slightly elongate the hole, creating an oval hole (photo n). The cord should be snug but able to be gently pulled through the slide.

14 Thread one end of the rubber cord through the tube bail. Even up the ends, and thread the ends in opposite directions through the slide (photo o).

15 Use superglue to adhere a bead with a 2mm hole on each cord end.

Millefiori corsage

In Italian, millefiori means "thousand flowers" and refers to a centuries-old glass-making technique. Adapted to polymer clay for this brooch, the technique's effect is dazzling

designed by **Jana Roberts Benzon**

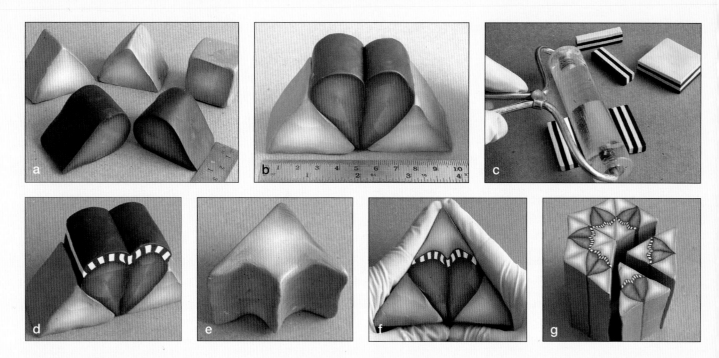

First developed by the glassblowers of the island of Murano in the Venetian lagoon, millefiori merges rods of colored glass into patterns and then stretches them out to form a cane. Millefiori glass cane-making techniques have been easily adapted to polymer clay and have gained popularity with a wide range of artisans making vessels, mosaics, and jewelry. The cane can be sliced, layered, and draped to produce many results, including this beautiful brooch.

Create a kaleidoscope cane

1 Make a Skinner blend using 3 oz. of gold clay and 3 oz. of ecru clay. Make a second Skinner blend using 1½ oz. of burgundy clay and 1½ oz. of gold. Cut each slab into a rectangle. Fold each rectangle in half lengthwise (the light-colored end will fold in half on itself and the dark-colored end will also fold in half on itself). Place one of the blends into the pasta machine, light end first. Run the slab through the pasta machine, beginning on the thickest setting and continuing to successively thinner settings up to a medium-thin setting. Repeat for the other blended slab.

2 Roll each slab, with the light-colored end of the slab at the center of each roll. Cut the gold roll into three 1¼-in. (3.2cm) pieces. Form two of the gold rolls into triangles. Use an acrylic block and roller to form the third gold roll into a square. Form each burgundy roll into a teardrop shape. Wrap the burgundy roll in a slab of dark brown clay rolled to the thin setting on the pasta machine. Cut the burgundy roll into two 1¼-in. pieces **(photo a)**.

3 Place the burgundy teardrops together so they form a heart shape. Indent one side of each of the gold triangles so that they fit snugly on each side of the burgundy heart **(photo b)**.

4 Make a two-colored tessellation: Condition 2 oz. of dark brown clay and 2 oz. of ecru. Run a 3½-in. (8.9cm) square slab of each through the pasta machine on the thickest setting. Cut a 3-in. (7.6cm) square slab from each sheet. Lay one slab on top of the other. Slice this stack in half, and lay one half on top of the other, creating a striped block. Use a tissue blade to cut five ⅛-in. (3mm)-thick slices from the striped block. Lay these five slices side by side on your work surface, and use a roller to meld the pieces into a striped slab **(photo c)**.

5 Run a slab of dark brown clay through the pasta machine on the thin setting. Lay the brown sheet on top of the striped slab, and trim it to fit. Set this layered slab on the heart, brown side up, and mark where cuts will be made so that it fits properly. Remove the layered slab, and place it on your work surface. Use a tissue blade to trim the layered slab and bevel the outer edges so that they will blend smoothly with the curve of the heart. Place the trimmed, layered slab back on the heart, and fit it into the crevice of the heart **(photo d)**.

6 Complete the triangle cane: Shape two of the corner edges of the square gold roll by grasping them and curving them downward **(photo e)**. Gently press this piece into place on top of the heart. Press all three sides of the triangle together so that the triangle has flat, equal sides **(photo f)**. Begin reducing the cane by holding it in one hand and slamming the three flat sides against a flat surface. Repeat several times on each side. This confirms the connection between the cane parts and warms the cane to help it stretch during reduction. Continue reducing the cane by following steps 1 and 2 of "Make the Corsage."

7 When the cane is reduced to ⅞ in. (2.2cm) evenly on each side, trim off the ragged ends, and cut the cane into six equal lengths. Arrange the sections on end, with a corner edge of each toward the center. Make sure to match up the tessellation on each cane with the adjacent canes. Once the kaleidoscope cane is together, it can be reduced further and formed into a circle, if desired **(photo g)**.

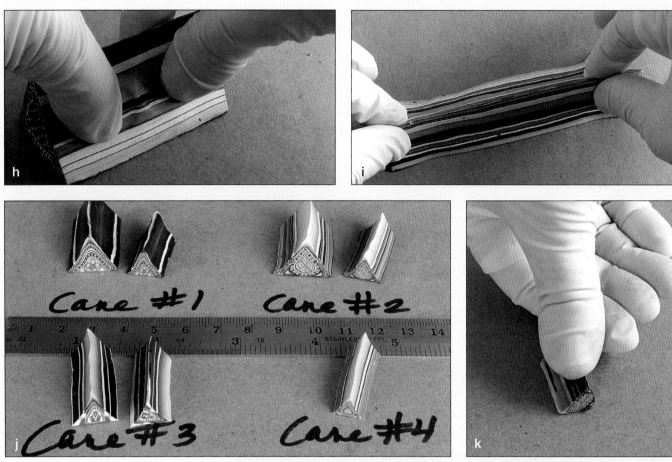

Make the corsage

1 Lengthen and reduce each triangular cane to a ¾-in. (1.9cm) side width and at least a 2-in. (5cm) length by pressing them with your thumb and forefinger, beginning in the center of each cane and moving toward the ends **(photo h)**. Turn and flip the cane often as you gently squeeze all the sides so that the entire cane receives the same amount of pressure. As the cane begins to lengthen, run your fingers along the cane to smooth and lengthen it. You will notice that the three corner edges do not reduce as quickly as the center. To coax the corner edges to lengthen, gently pull them with your thumb and fingers **(photo i)**. Use a gentle pinching movement along the corner edges to keep them crisp.

2 Assign each of your canes a number 1–4 **(photo j)**. From cane 1, cut a 1-in. (2.5cm) piece. Reduce the remaining cane to a side width of ½ in. (1.3cm), and cut a 1-in. piece. From cane 2, cut a 1-in. piece. Reduce the remaining cane to a side width of ½ in., and cut a 1-in. piece. Reduce cane 3 to a side

width of ½ in., and cut a 1-in. piece. Reduce the remaining cane to a side width of slightly larger than ⅜ in. (1cm), and cut a 1-in. piece. Reduce cane 4 to a side width of slightly larger than ⅜ in., and cut a 1-in. piece. Gently press in two of the bottom corner edges of each cane to form a teardrop shape **(photo k, l)**.

3 Condition 2 oz. of black clay, and run it through the pasta machine on the thinnest setting. Smooth the teardrop canes with your fingers, and wrap each one in a slab of black clay. Let the canes rest for 2 hours, or cool them quickly in the refrigerator for 30 minutes.

4 When assembling the brooch, work from the back to the front. The featured brooch has seven layers, with five slices in each layer. Form a ball of black clay ⅜ in. (9.5mm) in diameter, and press it down gently on a small ceramic-tile.
5 Cut five ¹⁄₁₆-in. (1.5mm) slices from each of the seven canes.
First layer: Arrange five ¾-in. (1.9cm) slices in a floral pattern around the clay ball with the points facing outward **(photo m)**.
Second layer: Place five ¾-in. slices staggered between the previous layer, with the points overlapping the clay ball **(photo n)**.

CANING

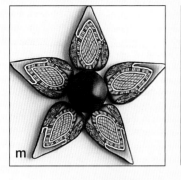

Third layer: Place five ½-in. (1.3cm) slices directly on top of the previous layer, with the points overlapping the clay ball.

Fourth layer: Place five ½-in. slices directly on top of the previous layer, with the points facing outward (photo o).

Fifth layer: Gently curve the points of the remaining ½-in. (1.3cm) slices downward before setting them in place. Place the five curved ½-in. slices staggered between the previous layer, with the points facing outward.

Sixth layer: Place five ⅜-in. (10mm) pieces staggered between the previous layer, with the points facing outward (photo p).

Seventh layer: The final five slices must be gently arched so the points slope downward. Place these five pieces staggered between the previous layer, with the points facing inward.

6 Use tweezers to pick up the rhinestones. Gently press one into the center and one on each of the five points of the first layer (photo q). Leave the rhinestones in place during baking. Bake the brooch on the ceramic tile according to the clay manufacturer's instructions.

7 After the brooch has cooled, dab a small amount of liquid clay on a pin

back. Press the pin back onto the back of the brooch. Run a small piece of black clay through the pasta machine on the thin setting. Cut out a disk from the slab that's ¾ in. (1.9cm) in diameter. Coat one side of the disk with a thin layer of liquid clay, place the disk on top of the opened pin back, and gently press the disk in place (photo r). Cut a slot in the side of a cardboard box only big enough to fit the pin back. Lay the brooch on top of the hole, with the pin back sitting inside the slot (photo s). This will help the brooch lie flat during baking. Bake the piece again with the box.

8 After the brooch has cooled, remove the rhinestones. Using tweezers to hold the rhinestones, apply a small drop of E6000 adhesive to the pointed backs of the rhinestones, and set them in place on the brooch.

supplies:

brooch, 1⅝ in. (4.1cm)

- polymer clay
  - 4 oz. black
  - 5 oz. ecru
  - 1½ oz. burgundy
  - 2 oz. dark brown
  - 5 oz. gold
- pointed-back rhinestones, **1** 12–20 stone size (ss), **5** 6–10 ss
- 1–1¼ in. (2.5–3.2cm) pin back
- pasta machine*
- tissue blade
- ruler
- acrylic block
- acrylic roller
- nonstick work surface
- tweezers
- small ceramic tile
- toaster oven*
- liquid polymer clay
- small cardboard box
- E6000 adhesive
- heating pad (optional)
- latex gloves (optional)

*Dedicated to use with polymer clay

Bobbin beads

Wind colorful polymer around sewing machine bobbins

designed by **Dotty McMillan**

a

b

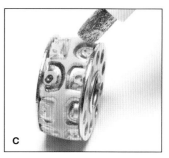

c

d

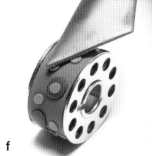

e

f

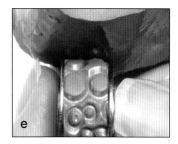

supplies:

bead, 13/16 in. (2.1cm)

- ½–1 oz. polymer clay in each of **1–3** colors
- steel sewing machine bobbin
- acrylic floor finish
- mica powder or gold-leafing pen (optional)
- craft brush
- needle tool
- pasta machine *
- texture sheets
- tissue blade
- toaster oven *
- spray bottle with water
- wet/dry sandpaper (400-grit)

*Dedicated to use with polymer clay

Choose which style or styles of beads you want to make. All start with the same base, and then you choose your desired surface treatment or inset. Condition each block of clay.

Base

1 Using ¼ oz. scrap or new clay of any color, set the pasta machine to the second-thickest setting, and roll a sheet about 4 in. (10cm) square.
2 Cut a strip of clay to measure the height of the cylinder in the center of the bobbin (⅜ in./1cm).
3 Wrap the strip around the center of the bobbin (**photo a**). Continue cutting strips and wrapping until the bobbin is filled to about ⅛ in. (3mm) from the edge. Press the clay firmly to smooth the seam and secure it without any gaps or air bubbles.
4 Repeat steps 1–3 for additional bobbins if desired.

Textured surface

1 Using about ¼ oz. of any color clay, set the pasta machine to the second-thickest setting, and roll a sheet that is about 4 in. square.
2 Spritz the texture sheet with water, and place it on the clay. Roll the texture sheet and clay through the pasta machine. Remove the texture sheet.
3 Cut a strip of textured clay as in step 2 of "Base," and wrap it around the prepared base of a bobbin. Trim the edges of the strip to meet (**photo b**). Smooth the edges, and retexture the seam if necessary, using a needle tool.

Metallic inset

1 Follow the instructions for "Textured surface."

2 Using a gold-leafing pen, trace the indentations (**photo c**), and let dry.
3 Using wet sandpaper, sand the clay to remove any unwanted marks.
4 Apply acrylic floor finish to seal the surface, and let dry.

Mica inset

1 Using about ¼ oz. of any color clay, set the pasta machine to the second-thickest setting, and roll a sheet that is about 4 in. square.
2 Using the craft brush, coat the surface of the clay with mica powder (**photo d**).
3 Texture the clay, wrap the bobbin, and bake as in steps 2–4 of "Textured surface."
4 Using wet sandpaper, sand the clay to remove the mica powder from the raised surface, leaving it in the indentations (**photo e**).
5 Apply acrylic floor finish to seal the surface, and let dry.

On-lay surface

1 Using about ¼ oz. of any color clay, set the pasta

machine to the second-thickest setting, and roll a sheet that is about 4 in. square.
2 Cut a strip of untextured clay, and wrap the bobbin as in steps 2 and 3 of "Base."
3 Decorate the outer strip of clay with small dots, stripes, swirls, shapes, or canes of clay in different colors (**photo f**).

Bake

Following the clay manufacturer's instructions, bake the bobbin assembly or assemblies in the toaster oven, and allow to cool completely.

Painting in miniature

Apply washes of
color to uncured
polymer clay
to create
picturesque jewelry

designed by **Patricia Kimle**

Taking a cue from miniature watercolor paintings, I applied transparent layers of alcohol-based inks to create the image on this polymer clay brooch. A thin overlay of translucent clay softens the crisp edges of the painting. The surface of the overlay is then sanded and buffed to give the brooch the look of glazed porcelain.

Pin

1 Roll a piece of scrap polymer clay ¼ in. (6mm) thick and slightly larger than a small oval cutter. Use the small oval cutter to cut an oval from the clay. Press the edges of the clay oval to bevel them a bit. This will distort the oval, so use the small oval cutter to cut the clay again to make a 1 x 2¼-in. (2.5 x 5.7cm) oval form **(photo a)**. Bake the form according to the clay manufacturer's instructions.
2 Condition the white, pearl, and translucent clays.
3 Make the front panel: Knead the white and pearl clay until the colors are blended. Roll the clay to ⅛ in. (3mm) thick. Use the large oval cutter to cut a 1¼ x 2½-in. (3.2 x 6.4cm) oval from the clay **(photo b)**.
4 Without cutting into the clay, use a blunt tool to lightly sketch the image onto the front panel **(photo c)**.
5 A sheet of glass set on top of white paper makes an excellent palette for mixing inks. The white paper allows you to accurately see the colors.
6 Apply a few drops of each ink color to the palette, keeping the colors at least 2 in. (5cm) apart. Allow the colors to dry.

7 Paint the foreground shape(s). Dip a round-tip paintbrush in isopropyl alcohol, and use the alcohol to dilute small amounts of ink. Mix colors to achieve the hue you'd like for the foreground image of your composition. The more alcohol you add to a color, the lighter and more transparent the color will appear. Fill in the foreground image with a solid wash of colored ink and alcohol **(photo d)**. Allow this base wash to dry.

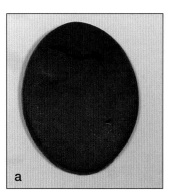

a

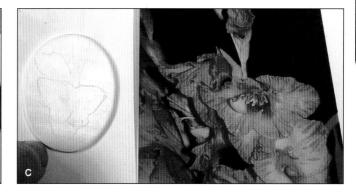

b

c

MIXED TECHNIQUES

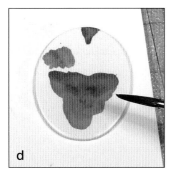

d

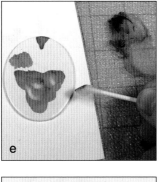

e

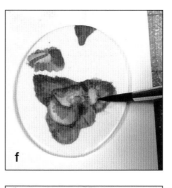

f

g

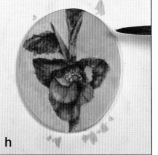

h

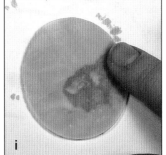

i

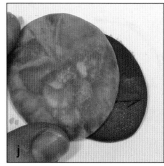

j

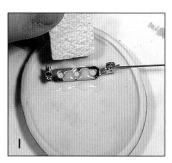

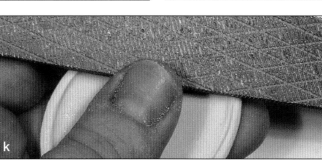

k

l

8 To create lighter areas in the base wash, dip the tip of a cotton swab in alcohol, and wipe away the color wash where you want a lighter value **(photo e)**.

9 Add details with darker values by filling your paint-brush with more ink than alcohol. Details and fine lines can be added with a fine-tip paintbrush **(photo f)**. Continue to define the details with crisp edges and clear shifts in value **(photo g)**, keeping in mind that the final image will be somewhat diffused by a layer of translucent clay.

10 Apply color washes to create the background, layering them as needed to add richness and to provide a sense of depth **(photo h)**. Working with a wet brush on a wet surface, "wet-in-wet," creates subtle color blends. For precise color separation, allow one application of color to dry before adding another layer of ink and alcohol. Allow the final wash to dry completely.

11 Use an acrylic roller to roll a very thin sheet of translucent clay. Use the large oval cutter to cut an oval from the translucent sheet. Lay the translucent oval on top of the painted panel and press down on it, working outward from the center to avoid trapping air bubbles between the clay layers **(photo i)**. To learn how to add gold-leaf inclusions to your translucent layer,

see "Add a Sliver of Shimmer," p. 69.

12 Shape the painted oval over the form. Use cornstarch as a release agent by brushing it on the back of the painted oval. Lay the painted oval, painted side up, over the beveled form to create a curved profile **(photo j)**. Bake the painted oval on the form according to the clay manufacturer's instructions. Allow the pieces to cool, and separate the painted oval from the form.

13 Use a flat hand file to file the back of the painted oval, beveling the edges and smoothing any imperfections **(photo k)**. Dip 400-grit wet/dry sandpaper in water and lightly sand the front of the painted oval. Progress to 600- and then 800-grit

sandpaper, being careful not to sand through the thin layer of translucent clay. Polish the surface with a muslin buff on a buffing wheel.

14 Place an open pin-back finding on the back of the painted oval. Apply liquid polymer clay to the pin back and then cover the pin back with a thin sheet of clay to secure the finding **(photo l)**. Check to ensure that the pin stem closes properly. Bake the piece again.

EDITOR'S NOTE:
For a crackle effect, place gold or silver leaf onto a layer of white clay. Use a roller over the clay to "crackle" the leaf. Then paint your image onto a thin layer of translucent clay. Place the painting, ink side down, onto the crackled leaf.

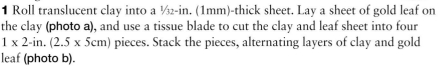

supplies:

brooch, 2¼ x 1¾ in. (5.7 x 4.4cm)

- polymer clay
  - ½ oz. white
  - ½ oz. pearl
  - ½ oz. translucent
- alcohol-based ink
- gold leaf: 24k or imitation (optional)
- pin-back finding
- liquid polymer clay
- pasta machine*
- oval cutters: 1 x 2¼ in. (2.5 x 5.7cm), 1¼ x 2½ in. (3.2 x 6.4cm); or two same-shaped cutters, one slightly smaller than the other
- toaster oven*
- nonstick work surface
- blunt tool
- glass sheet: 8 x 11 in. (20 x 28cm)
- paintbrushes: round tip, fine tip
- isopropyl alcohol
- cotton swabs
- acrylic roller
- tissue blade (optional)
- waxed paper (optional)
- cornstarch
- hand files
- wet/dry sandpaper (400-, 600-, 800-grit)
- buffing wheel, muslin buff

*Dedicated to use with polymer clay

Add a sliver of shimmer

Adding slivers of 24k or imitation gold leaf to the translucent clay overlay will give the polymer a bit of shine. A little shimmer goes a long way, so use this layering technique sparingly to give the overlay of clay a pattern that looks like wood grain.

1 Roll translucent clay into a ⅟₃₂-in. (1mm)-thick sheet. Lay a sheet of gold leaf on the clay **(photo a)**, and use a tissue blade to cut the clay and leaf sheet into four 1 x 2-in. (2.5 x 5cm) pieces. Stack the pieces, alternating layers of clay and gold leaf **(photo b)**.

2 Cut the stack in half **(photo c)**, and stack the halves to make a square stack.

3 Apply pressure to compress the layers of clay **(photo d)**. Using a tissue blade, cut through the stack, starting at the upper right corner and slicing diagonally down to the lower left corner **(photo e)**.

4 Restack the clay. Restack the two slices of clay so that the bottom piece is now on top **(photo f)**. Roll the stack with an acrylic roller to compress the clay.

5 Add slices to a translucent clay sheet. Roll 1 oz. of translucent clay into a ⅟₁₆-in. (1.5mm)-thick sheet. Holding the tissue blade nearly horizontal to the stack, shave thin slices from the top and lay them on the clay sheet **(photo g)**. Roll the slices flat with the roller.

6 Fold a piece of waxed paper in half, and feed it fold-first approximately 1 in. into the pasta machine set to the thinnest setting. Hold the clay sheet vertically, and insert it between the paper. Run the clay through the pasta machine, allowing the clay and paper to pass through the rollers at independent rates. The paper prevents the clay from adhering to the rollers. The clay will stretch and get very thin. Peel the clay from the paper.

7 Place this sheet of clay over the front of the brooch, keeping the gold-leaf flecks against the painted surface.

a

b

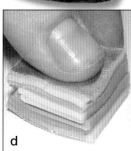

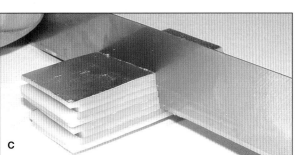

c

d

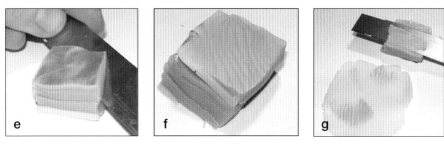

e

f

g

June bug

This fun polymer clay scarab is cute as a button … or brooch or pendant

designed by **Lori Wilkes**

To start this project, make simple bull's-eye, striped, or checkerboard canes in your chosen color schemes.

Bug's abdomen and wings

1 To form the abdomen, roll an egg-shaped ball of any color clay about 1¼ x ⅞ in. (3.2 x 2.2cm), and flatten one side for the bottom **(photo a)**.

2 Using a tissue blade, cut thin slices from a bull's-eye, striped, or checkerboard cane. Apply the slices to cover the top surface of the abdomen **(photo b)**. Take care to avoid air bubbles, smooth any seams, and trim excess clay.

3 Set the pasta machine to the thickest setting, cut about ¼ oz. of any color clay, and roll it through the pasta machine. Carefully lay a metal foil sheet on top of the clay, and gently burnish it with your fingertip. Remove excess foil sheet. Decrease the thickness of the setting, and roll the clay through again. Roll the clay through the pasta machine two more times, decreasing the thickness of the setting each time to crackle the foil and imbed it in the clay **(photo c)**.

4 To form the hind wings, cut two strips of crackled foil clay the length of the abdomen, and place them along each side of the abdomen, allowing the previous layer to show in the center and making the ends touch at the tail. Use an acrylic roller to gently press each wing to remove air bubbles. Trim any excess clay **(photo d)**.

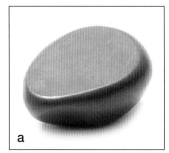

a

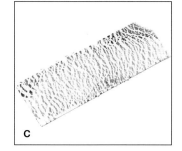

b

c

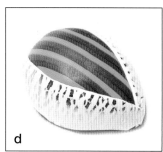

d

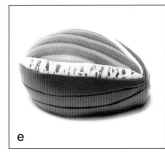

e

f

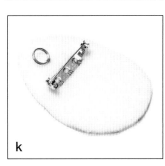

g

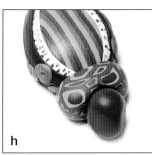

h

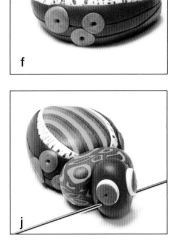

i

j

k

5 Set the pasta machine to the thin setting, and roll a sheet of any color clay. To form the forewings, cut two strips the length of the abdomen, and place them on top of the hind wings, allowing a strip of hind wing to show on each side. Use an acrylic roller to remove air bubbles, and trim as in step 4. Using the needle tool, draw a few lines like stripes along the length of the forewings **(photo e)**.

6 To make wing spots, roll six balls of any color clay about 1/16 in. (2mm) or smaller, and flatten them into disks. Place them on the sides of the forewings near the rounded end of the abdomen, and press the ball-end tool into the center of each disk to form an indentation **(photo f)**.

7 With the tissue blade slightly curved, trim the rounded end of the abdomen **(photo g)**.

Thorax and head

1 To form the thorax, roll a ball of any color clay about 7/8 x 1/2 in. (3.2 x 1.3cm).

2 Using the tissue blade, cut thin slices from a bull's-eye

cane. Apply the slices to cover the clay ball, and roll the ball to smooth the edges. Gently form the ball into an disk, flatten two sides, and press it onto the trimmed edge of the abdomen.

3 To form the head, roll a ball of any color clay about 3/8 in. (1cm) diameter. Press the head onto the thorax, and slightly indent the clay where the eyes will be placed **(photo h)**.

4 To make eyes, roll two balls of any color clay about 1/8 in. (3mm) diameter, and flatten them into disks. Using a contrasting color of clay, roll two balls about 1/16 in. (2mm) diameter, and flatten them into disks. Stack the smaller disks on top of the larger disks, and press each stacked disk onto the pinched areas for the eyes. Press the ball end tool into the center of each disk stack. Use the needle tool to gently press little dots all over the head for texture.

5 To make a hole to guide the antennae wire, use the needle tool to pierce a hole through the head, behind the eyes near the base **(photo i)**.

Baking and finishing

1 Following the clay manufacturer's instructions, bake the bug in the toaster oven, taking into account the thickness of the clay (see Editor's Note, p. 72). Allow the bug to cool completely.

2 Paint the indentations and lines made with the ball end and needle tools with acrylic paint **(photo j)**, and use a paper towel to wipe off any excess. Let the paint dry.

3 Use a paintbrush to apply acrylic floor finish to the hind wings, and let dry.

Beadwork and assembly

1 Trace the shape of the bug onto the foundation, leaving about 1/4 in. (6mm) around the edges, and cut out the shape. Tie an overhand knot on one end of 18 in. (46cm) of thread, and sew up through the foundation. Sew the pin-back finding securely to the foundation. Center the soldered jump ring or split ring above the pin back, and sew it securely to the foundation. End the thread **(photo k)**.

2 If necessary, sand the bottom of the bug. Tape

supplies:

sculpted brooch/pendant, 1½ x 2½ in. (3.8 x 6.4cm)

- polymer clay 1–2 oz. in each of **6–9** colors
- 2–3g 6° seed beads
- 1–2g 11° seed beads
- 3 in. (7.6cm) 22-gauge craft wire
- 6mm soldered jump ring or split ring
- pin-back finding
- nylon beading thread, size D
- beading needles, #10 or #12
- acrylic paint, 2–3 colors
- acrylic roller
- ball-end clay tool
- double-sided tape or E6000 adhesive
- 3 in. (7.6cm) square felt or Lacy's Stiff Stuff beading foundation
- acrylic floor finish
- metal foil sheet (gold, silver, or copper)
- needle tool
- paintbrush
- paper towel
- pasta machine*
- sandpaper (100-grit)
- scissors
- tissue blade
- toaster oven*
- 3-in. (7.6cm) square Ultrasuede
- chainnose pliers
- roundnose pliers
- wire cutters

*Dedicated to use with polymer clay

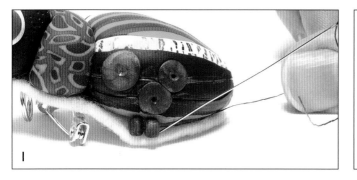

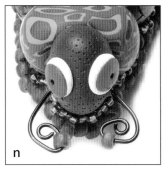

FIGURE 1

foundation

FIGURE 2

or glue the bug to the foundation. If using E6000 adhesive, allow the glue to dry for 15 minutes. Trim the foundation to ⅛–¼ in. (3–6mm) around the edges.

3 To add beaded trim around the base of the bug, tie an overhand knot on one end of 2 yd. (1.8 m) of thread, and sew up through the foundation next to the bug. Pick up two 6º seed beads, lay them along the edge of the bug, and sew down through the foundation next to the end of the second 6º **(figure 1, a–b and photo l)**. Sew up through the

foundation next to the first 6º **(b–c)**, and sew through both 6ºs again **(c–d)**.

4 Pick up two 6ºs, and sew down through the foundation **(d–e)**. Sew up through the foundation between the two 6ºs in the previous stitch **(e–f)**, sew through one 6º from the previous stitch and the two new 6ºs **(f–g)**. Continue working in beaded backstitch **(g–h)** around the base of the bug, keeping each pair of 6ºs as close to the previous pair of 6ºs as possible without making them bunch together.

5 To add picot trim, sew up through the foundation between a 6º and the bug. Pick up three 11º seed beads, and, leaving a space the width of two 11ºs, sew down through the foundation **(figure 2, a–b)**. Sew up through the foundation next to the first 11º, and sew through the first and third 11ºs **(b–c)**. Repeat around the base of the bug.

6 To add picot trim below the round of 6ºs, sew through the foundation between a 6º and the foundation, repeat step 5, and end the thread.

7 Cut a piece of Ultrasuede to fit the bottom of the bug, and cut openings for the pin back and jump ring **(photo m)**. Tape or glue the Ultrasuede to the foundation. Whip stitch the edges together if desired.

8 Cut a 3-in. (7.6cm) piece of craft wire, and center it in the hole behind the eyes. Bend the wire ends up where they exit the holes, add optional 6ºs to the ends, and use chainnose and roundnose pliers to curl the ends toward the center of the head **(photo n)**.

EDITOR'S NOTE:

To avoid scorching your bug in the oven, make a tent with aluminum foil, and place it over the top of the bug while baking. The bug will most likely be thicker than the recommended thickness on the clay's package. Instead of adding together the stated baking times and baking all at once, bake for the minimum amount of time in several increments, allowing the clay to cool between sessions.

Mixed-media links

Combine easy
forging and
soldering, woven
wire, and polymer
clay to make
bold links

designed by **Desiree McCrorey**

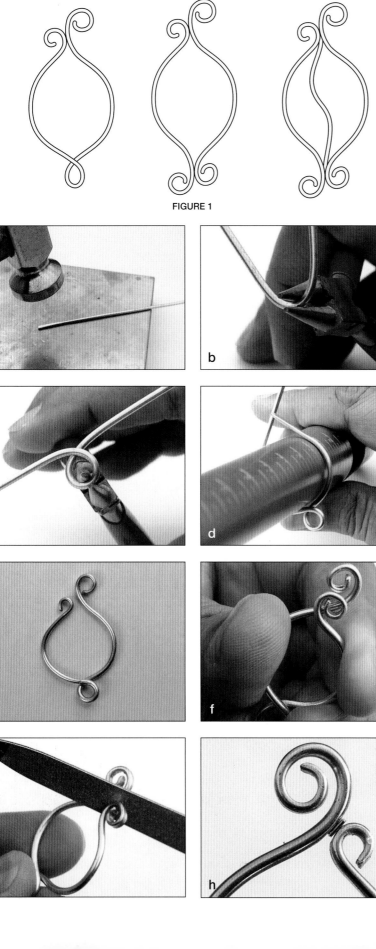

ONE-WIRE FRAME   TWO-WIRE FRAME   THREE-WIRE FRAME

FIGURE 1

With three different paisley-shaped links and four ways to embellish them, this bracelet is loaded with options. To give the links extra color and texture, you can apply pigments to create a patina, impress the clay with patterns, and embed bits of wire or other metal pieces into the clay.

Making the frames

The featured bracelet is composed of a one-wire frame, a two-wire frame, and two three-wire frames (figure 1).

One-wire frame

1 Cut a 4-in. (10cm) piece of 14-gauge brass wire and use 400-grit sandpaper to smooth the ends. Place the wire on a steel block and use a planishing hammer to flatten the ends (photo a).

2 Use roundnose pliers to grasp the wire 1⅞ in. (4.8cm) from one end, and bend the wire into a V (photo b). (For a symmetrical link, grasp the wire at its midpoint.) Push the wire ends past each other, creating a loop (photo c). Bend the wire around a ring mandrel or PVC pipe (photo d). Use roundnose pliers to make a loop on each end (photo e).

3 Squeeze the link, pushing the ends past each other (photo f). Let the ends spring back until they touch. Use 400-grit sandpaper or a file to create a flat spot where the ends touch (photo g).

4 Place a pallion of hard solder between the ends where they touch. The tension between the work-hardened ends will hold the solder in place (photo h). Flux the frame and place it on your soldering surface. Use a handheld butane torch to heat the entire frame with a soft, bushy flame. Then aim the flame toward the solder until it flows (photo i). Quench and pickle the frame.

5 After being pickled, brass tends to acquire a zinc depletion plating that causes the surface to appear a coppery color. You can remove the plating by placing the frame in a solution of 50 percent pickle and 50 percent hydrogen peroxide. Or, you can use steel wool to remove any depletion plating or oxidation. Rinse and dry the frame (photo j).

Two-wire frame

1 Prepare and shape the wires. Cut a 2¾-in. (7cm) piece and a 3¼-in. (8.3cm) piece of 14-gauge wire, and file the ends smooth. Use roundnose pliers to make a loop at each end so that the loops curl toward each other **(photo k)**. Press the center of each wire against a ring mandrel to bow it **(photo l)**. Use a marker to indicate the points where each wire touches the other. File these points flat with a #2-cut, flat hand file.
2 Flux the wires, place them on your soldering surface, and heat the entire frame. Use a soldering pick to place hard solder where the wires meet **(photo m)**. Torch the frame until the solder flows. Quench, pickle, rinse, and dry the frame.
3 To make the frame fit more comfortably on your wrist, lay the frame perpendicularly on a bracelet mandrel and tap the frame lightly with a rawhide mallet to create a slight curve. (You can substitute a PVC pipe or rolling pin for the mandrel.) Use steel wool to remove any remaining oxidation or rough areas.

Three-wire frames

1 Cut two pieces of wire as you did to make the two-wire frame, and file the ends smooth. Cut a 1½-in. (3.8cm) piece of wire, and file the ends to a V.
2 Follow the instructions for the two-wire frame to shape the two longer wires. Make a slight curve in the shortest wire, and place it so that its ends fit snugly between the points where the two longer wires meet.
3 Flux and heat the entire frame. Use a soldering pick to place hard solder where the wires meet **(photo n)**. Torch, quench, pickle, rinse, and dry the frame.
4 Contour the frames. Create a slight curve in the frame as you did for the two-wire frame. Use steel wool to remove any remaining oxidation or rough areas **(photo o)**. Make another three-wire frame.

Filling the frames
One-wire frame: polymer clay

1 Condition the pearl-colored polymer clay. To imitate ivory, mix equal amounts of ecru and translucent polymer clay, and then mix in a tiny amount of yellow ochre.

supplies:

bracelet, 8½ x 1¼ in. (20 x 3.2cm)
- polymer clay
  - pearl, copper, or other
  - ecru, translucent, yellow ochre (optional)
- brass or sterling silver wire
  - 25 in. (64cm) 14-gauge, dead-soft
  - 24 in. (61cm) 24-gauge, dead-soft
  - 9¼ ft. (2.8m) 26-gauge, dead-soft
- brass wire, scraps, and pins
- acrylic paint: burnt umber (optional)
- 8–10 14-gauge jump rings, 5mm inside diameter
- brass toggle clasp
- wire cutters
- wet/dry sandpaper (400-, 600-, 1000-grit)
- emery file (optional)
- steel block
- planishing hammer
- rawhide mallet
- roundnose pliers
- chainnose pliers
- mandrels: ring, bracelet; PVC pipe or rolling pin (optional)
- soldering station: torch, solder (hard), fire-resistant surface (soldering pad, fire brick, or charcoal block), pickle pot with pickle, flux, copper tongs, pick; hydrogen peroxide (optional)
- steel wool (0000)
- permanent marker
- hand file: #2-cut flat
- nonstick work surface
- acrylic roller
- craft knife or tissue blade
- 2 wooden dowels
- needle tool or toothpick
- clay-sculpting tools
- vise with protected jaws
- toaster oven*
- paintbrush (optional)

*Dedicated to use with polymer clay

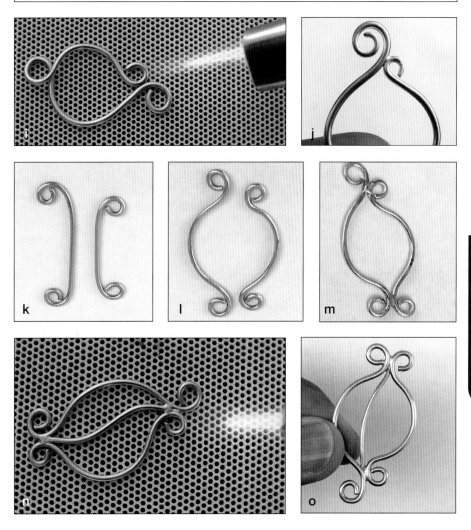

MIXED TECHNIQUES

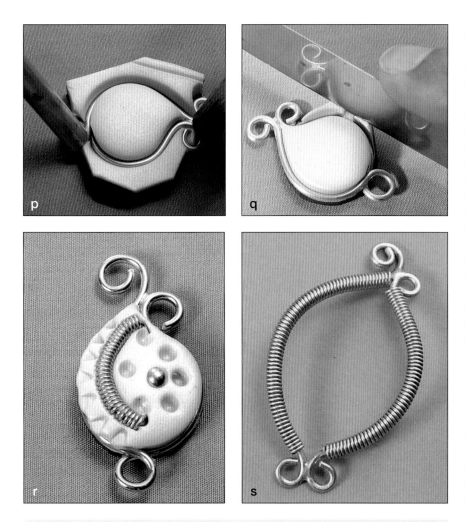

2 Use an acrylic roller to roll a ⅛-in. (3mm)-thick slab of clay. Cut the slab into three rectangles that are slightly longer and wider than the one-wire frame. Layer the rectangles to make a stack.

3 Place the frame on the stack of clay. Use a dowel at each end of the frame to press the frame into the clay, but don't break through the bottom of the stack **(photo p)**. Use a tissue blade or craft knife to remove the excess clay around the frame **(photo q)**. Remove the clay in the loops using a needle tool or toothpick.

4 Insert bits of brass wire, brass pins, or other scraps into the clay. Make indentations in the clay with sculpting tools or needle files. Allow the clay to spread slightly beyond the frame **(photo r)**. This helps to prevent the clay from separating from the frame. Set the link aside.

Two-wire frame: polymer clay and wire wrap

1 Cut 24 in. (61cm) of 24-gauge brass wire. Avoiding the loops, wrap the wire around the frame, leaving a very slight space between the wraps **(photo s)**. Trim the excess wire.

2 Press the frame into a stack of polymer clay. The slight spaces between the wire wraps will grip the clay and hold it in place. Use a needle tool to remove excess clay from the loops. Add embedments and texture to the clay, and set aside the two-wire frame.

Three-wire frame: half polymer clay and half wire weave

1 Clamp the lower half of a three-wire frame in a vise. Cut a 39-in. (1m) piece of 26-gauge brass wire. Leaving a 1-in. (2.5cm) tail, wrap one end of the working wire around the top center wire of the frame. Weave the working wire in a figure-8 pattern, wrapping the center frame wire and one outside frame wire **(figure 2)**. Stop weaving when you reach the widest point in the frame **(photo t)**, and then remove the frame from the vise. Flip the frame over, clamp it in the vise, and continue weaving to the end of the frame **(photo u)**. Cut the wire, leaving a 1-in. tail.

2 Place the open half of the frame on a stack of polymer clay **(photo v)**, and press the frame into the clay. Use a craft knife or tissue blade to remove excess clay from the frame **(photo w)**, and use a needle tool

HALF AND HALF:
Of the three frame styles, the three-wire design is the most versatile, because you can incorporate polymer clay and woven wire in one link. Experiment with links filled only with polymer clay. Fill half of the frame with polymer clay and bake it according to the manufacturer's instructions. Fill the remaining half with a contrasting color and bake it again.

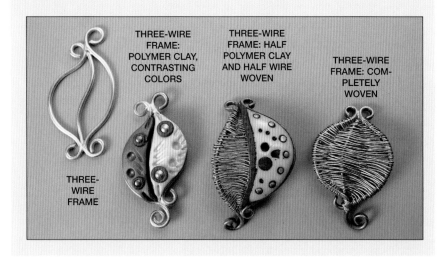

THREE-WIRE FRAME

THREE-WIRE FRAME: POLYMER CLAY, CONTRASTING COLORS

THREE-WIRE FRAME: HALF POLYMER CLAY AND HALF WIRE WOVEN

THREE-WIRE FRAME: COMPLETELY WOVEN

to remove clay from the loops and woven wire.

3 Wrap the tails around the frame a few times, and trim the excess wire. Use chainnose pliers to tuck the tails into the weave.

4 Bake the links according to the clay manufacturer's instructions. For finishing ideas, see "Surface treatments," below.

Three-wire frame: completely woven

1 Clamp the lower half of the other three-wire frame in a vise. Cut a 6-ft. (1.8m) piece of 26-gauge brass wire. Leaving a 1-in. tail, wrap the working wire around the top center wire of the frame. Use an under-and-over weave to wrap the working wire across all three frame wires. When you reach the frame's widest point, remove it from the vise.

2 Clamp the woven half of the frame in the vise and continue weaving to the end of the frame. Trim and tuck the tails. To see all the options for filling a three-wire frame, see "Half and Half," left.

Assembly

Connect the links with 14-gauge brass jump rings. Use a jump ring to attach half of the toggle clasp to one end of the bracelet. Repeat on the other end.

Surface treatments

1 Give baked clay a smooth surface by sanding it with progressively finer grits of sandpaper.

2 Coat baked and sanded clay with burnt umber acrylic paint to give the clay a weathered patina. Before the paint dries, use a paper towel to remove excess pigment, leaving some paint in the indentations and embedments to emphasize the texture. Rebake the clay, and then sand the surface with 1000-grit sandpaper.

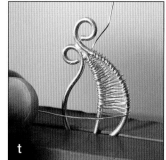

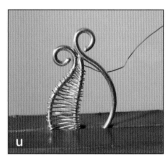

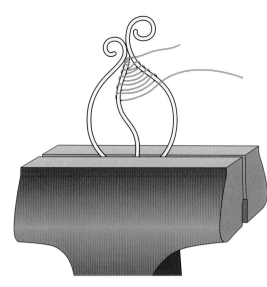

FIGURE 2

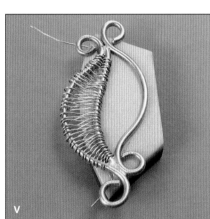

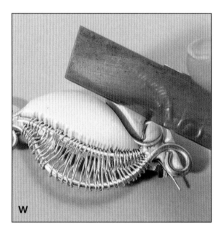

MIXED TECHNIQUES

Cross-pollination

Cultivate a variety of techniques to build a hybrid pod pendant

designed by **Jeffrey Lloyd Dever**

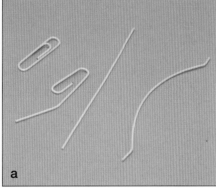

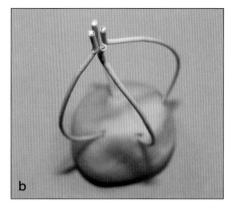

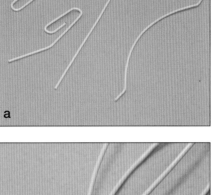

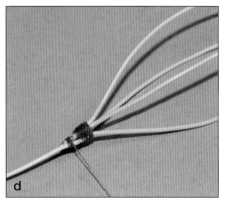

Woven frame

1 Straighten four plastic-coated paper clips, taking care not to damage the coating. Use nylon-jaw pliers to remove any kinks. Use wire cutters to cut the four wires into 3-in. (7.6cm) pieces. Bend a gentle curve in each wire.

2 Measure ³⁄₁₆ in. (5mm) from one end of a wire and make a 45-degree bend. Repeat to bend the other end of the wire **(photo a)**. Repeat for the remaining three wires.

3 Insert one end of each wire into a base of uncured scrap clay **(photo b)**. The exposed wire ends should be slightly stepped to form a tapered tip. Use thread to tightly wrap the wire ends together.

4 After you've made several wraps, hold the working thread taut and apply a drop of superglue, letting it soak into the thread wrapping. Use the corner of a tissue to blot any excess glue. Allow the glue to dry completely, and trim the thread tail. For tips on using instant glues, see "Stick to These Glue Guidelines," p. 82.

5 Remove the wires from the clay. Wrap, glue, and trim the other end of the frame **(photo c)**. You'll have a four-sided frame that is tapered at the ends.

NOTE: If the glued thread is rough and lumpy, use 100-grit sandpaper to smooth the glue's surface. Be careful not to sand through the thread, or the join will fail. You can also use 100-grit sandpaper to shape the protruding wire ends into a smooth, tapered point.

6 Cut a 96-in. (2.44m) piece of 24-gauge plastic-coated copper wire. This will be your weaving wire. Position one end of the weaving wire against the glued thread at one end of the pod frame. (The weaving wire will look like a stem for the frame.) Use thread to make three or four wraps to secure the weaving wire to the frame **(photo d)**. Apply a drop of superglue to the thread and allow the glue to dry completely.

MIXED TECHNIQUES

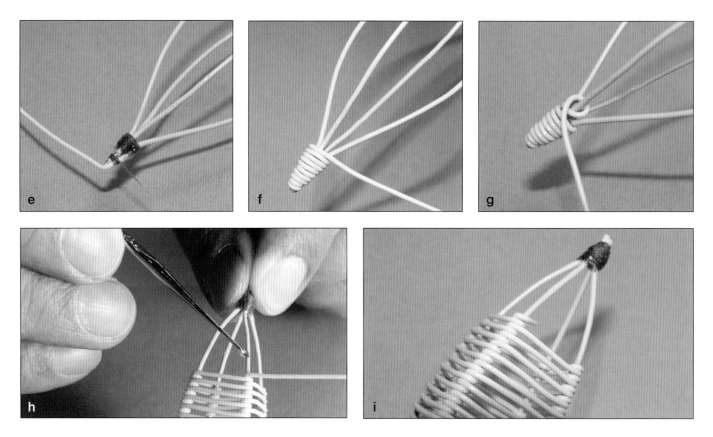

7 Grasp the weaving wire just below its connection to the frame. Bend the weaving wire perpendicular to the frame **(photo e)**. Trim the thread tail. Working counterclockwise, gently wrap the weaving wire tightly around the tip of the frame, covering the glued thread **(photo f)**. When you reach the portion of the frame where the ribs begin to branch out, stop wrapping and secure the weaving wire to the frame with a drop of glue.

8 Weave the wire onto the frame. When the glue is completely dry, you'll use the weaving wire to make a basket weave pattern with the ribs of the frame.

TIP: When you're working with long pieces of wire, wear eye protection, and give yourself plenty of room to manipulate the wire. Work slowly to avoid tangles.

9 Working counterclockwise, loop the weaving wire around the closest rib **(photo g)**. Rotate the frame, and loop the weaving wire around the next rib. Keeping the weaving wire taut, but not so tight that it deforms the frame,

continue to work around and up the frame.

10 Periodically compress the wraps along the ribs and toward your starting wraps. As you work along the frame, you can use a #12 crochet hook to intermittently apply a drop of glue to stabilize the weaving **(photo h)**. Allow the glue to dry completely before you continue weaving.

11 Weave until you've covered three-quarters of the frame's length. Cut the weaving wire, leaving a ¼-in. (6.5mm) tail. Tuck the tail toward the center of the frame **(photo i)**, and secure the tail with a drop of glue.

Polymer clay cap

1 Condition and blend 2 oz. of yellow clay, 2 oz. of white clay, and a pinch of lime green clay, and run it through the pasta machine set to a medium-thin setting.
2 Press the clay over the unwoven end of the frame **(photo j)**, shaping the clay to conform to the contours of the ribs.
3 Place the assembly on a thin layer of polyester fiberfill. Cover the assembly with a piece of tented aluminum foil to

prevent the clay from getting scorched and the wires from being damaged during baking. Bake the assembly according to the clay manufacturer's instructions. (For tips on baking clay, see "Prevent Scorching," p. 83.)

NOTE: For all subsequent baking, set the clay assembly on a polyester fiberfill support and cover the clay with tented aluminum foil.

4 After the assembly has cooled completely, use 100-grit sandpaper to refine the cap's base. (I use dry sand-papers to refine my work because they help me see any imperfections. Then I use a baby wipe to remove any dust.)

NOTE: The safest way to avoid inhaling polymer dust while sanding is to use wet/dry sandpaper and sand the piece under water. If you choose to dry-sand your piece, work in a well-ventilated area and wear a dust mask.

5 Run the clay that's left over from the blend you mixed for the base through a pasta machine set to its thickest setting.

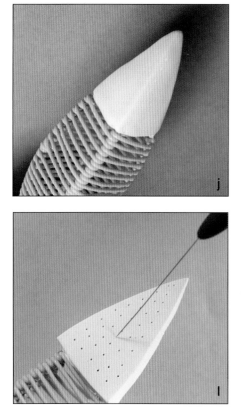

MAKE YOUR OWN MICRO-NEEDLE TOOL

This micro-needle tool made from a beading needle is perfect for making hair-thin holes in polymer clay. Dip the eye of a #15 needle into a drop of liquid polymer clay, insert the eye into a small piece of uncured polymer clay for the handle, and bake. Easy!

6 Use a craft knife or tissue blade to cut out a triangle of clay that is slightly larger than one side of the base. Position this veneer of clay over one side of the base, leaving about an ⅛-in. (3mm) lip of clay overhanging the tip and short side of the triangle (photo k).

7 Gently press the veneer against the base, and use a tissue blade to trim the excess clay so that the veneer is flush with the edges of the base.

8 Repeat to add a veneer to the remaining sides of the base, being sure to apply each triangle of clay adjacent to the previous veneered side. Overlap and trim the clay veneer to give the cap clean edges and sturdy joins.

9 Without deforming the clay, gently pinch the edges of the cap together. Smooth the joins with your fingertip.

10 When you layer uncured clay over a cured surface, air may get trapped between the layers. This air causes unsightly bubbles to form during baking. To prevent these bubbles from forming, use a needle tool to pierce tiny vent holes through the uncured clay down to the cured layer (photo l).

11 Moisten your fingertip with water, and gently stroke it over the surface of the clay to close the holes. (I've found that saliva works best!)

NOTE: These steps may be enough to work out any trapped air. If some air remains trapped, the surface with the healed holes is weak enough to allow the air to escape as the clay cures.

12 Bake the piece using the polyester fiberfill and aluminum foil tent. Allow the assembly to cool completely.

13 Wrap masking tape around the frame. Use 100-grit sandpaper to shape the clay cap, keeping the edges sharp and well defined (photo m). Use a baby wipe to remove all the dust from the surface of the cap. Set the assembly aside to dry completely. Remove the masking tape from the frame.

14 Select two colors to make a Skinner blend. I made the first color for my blend by mixing 1 oz. of red pearl clay with 1 oz. of gold pearl clay. My second color is 2 oz. of pearl mixed with ½ oz. of gold pearl.

15 Run the blend through the pasta machine on progressively thinner settings, stopping after you've run it through the thin setting. Set this veneer aside to cool and firm up.

MIXED TECHNIQUES

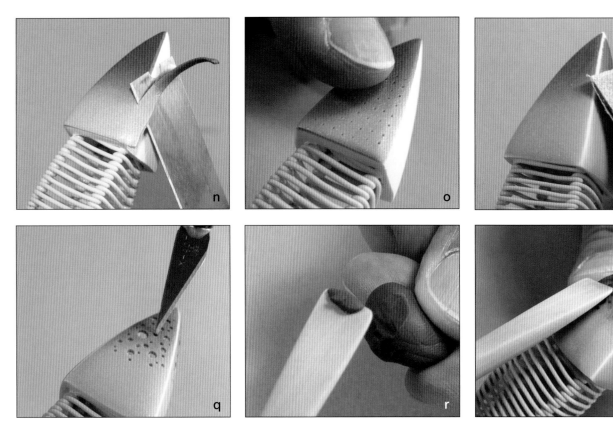

STICK TO THESE GLUE GUIDELINES:

Superglues come in a variety of viscosities, and each may have a different cure time. Generally, the thicker glues dry more slowly than the thinner ones. I prefer the quick-drying variety. When you're using superglues, keep the following in mind:

- Work in a well-ventilated area. Try not to inhale the glue's fumes.
- Apply hand cream before you use the glue, and keep baby wipes handy for cleaning up any mishaps.
- Wear eye protection, and avoid positioning your head directly over the area you are gluing.
- To apply glue with precision, place a few drops on a piece of aluminum foil. Dip the end of a #12 crochet hook into the glue, allowing capillary action between the glue and the crochet hook to hold the glue in place until you touch it to the application site.
- Use gravity to your advantage—let the glue flow away from you.
- Always allow glue to dry completely before you expose it to oven temperatures. Make sure to use the oven in a well-ventilated area.

16 Cut out a section of the blend veneer that is slightly larger than one side of the cap. Gently apply the veneer to one side of the cap, being careful not to trap air.

17 Use your fingertip to smooth and burnish the veneer so that it makes a firm bond with the cap. Use your tissue blade to trim the excess veneer from the three edges of this side of the cap (photo n).

18 Use your micro-needle tool to pierce the uncured clay with closely spaced holes across the entire surface of the veneer. Moisten your fingertip with water and gently stroke the surface of the veneer to heal the holes (photo o).

19 Use your tissue blade to refine the edges of the veneer. Bake.

20 Repeat to apply the remaining three veneer panels, adding them one at a time and baking the assembly before you add the next veneer panel.

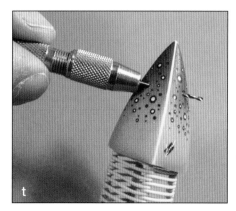

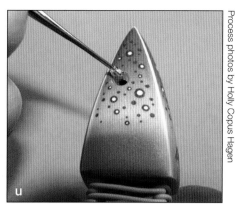

Process photos by Holly Copus Hagen

Refining

1 When the assembly is cool, use 220-grit sandpaper to smooth the surface of the cap and refine its edges (photo p). Use a light touch, removing just enough of the top veneer to reveal the desired area of the underlying layer of clay. I sanded the edges of the cap just enough to reveal a slender stripe at each corner.

2 Use the tip of your craft knife to carve a random pattern of various-sized holes in the cap (photo q).

TIP: Before you make holes in the pendant, practice making holes in a tile of cured scrap clay. Use a new blade, and rotate the craft knife with light, even pressure as if you were using a pin-vise drill.

3 When you've finished making the holes, blow out the shavings and use a soft-bristle toothbrush to sweep away any remaining clay debris.

4 Select a contrasting color of clay to backfill the holes. (I chose a dark purple.) Use a square-tip wooden shaping tool to pick up a small amount of clay (photo r). Spread the clay across the surface of the cap, filling the holes (photo s).

5 Without pulling the uncured clay out of the holes, scrape away the excess clay. I use a baby wipe to compress the uncured clay into the holes and to remove any remaining residue from the surface of the cap. Bake and let cool.

6 To give the cap more visual pop, use the tip of the craft knife to make holes in the center of several of the backfilled circles. Then, backfill these small holes with some of the leftover clay from the base. One last baking session and the cap is ready to finish.

Finishing

1 After the assembly has cooled, tape off the frame of the pendant to protect it during the finishing process. Put on your dust mask. Use 220-grit sandpaper with a light touch to smooth the surface of the cap. Then switch to 00000 steel wool, moving it in a circular motion with light pressure over the cap's surface. Use a baby wipe to remove any dust.

2 To give the cap's surface a low-gloss sheen, gently hand-polish it with a soft lint-free cloth. For a glossier surface, sand the cap with progressively higher grit sandpapers and carefully polish it on a buffing machine.

3 Use a pin vise with a 1.5mm drill bit to make a pilot hole through the cap. Using light pressure, slowly drill all the way through the cap (photo t).

4 Insert a slightly larger bit into the pilot hole. To avoid chipping or cracking the top veneer, drill just halfway into the cap. Then remove the bit, insert it into the other side of the pilot hole, and again drill just halfway into the cap. Repeat this process, using progressively larger bits, until you've drilled a hole

PREVENT SCORCHING:

When you're curing a piece made of polymer clay a number of times, it's best to take some precautions to prevent scorching (which can release unhealthy fumes).

Light colors of clay (pearl and translucent in particular) are susceptible to browning. To prevent the clay from burning, place a thin layer of polyester fiberfill underneath your piece and an aluminum foil tent above it.

Pay particular attention when you're putting your piece in the oven to bake. Make sure that your assembly does not come in contact with the heating elements above or below it.

Monitor the temperature with a stand-alone thermometer. Make sure the oven holds the heat at the recommended temperature.

large enough to fit your cable (I used an anodized niobium cable) and to allow the pendant to move freely.

5 To reinforce the hole, dip the end of a #12 crochet hook into a drop of super-glue. Use the crochet hook to carefully apply a thin coat of glue to the interior wall of the hole openings (photo u). Allow the glue to dry overnight, and then string the pendant on your cable.

MIXED TECHNIQUES

Polymer and metal clay earrings

Polymer clay makes a colorful backdrop for fine-silver metal clay components. Whether you make these earrings as dangles or with embedded studs, you'll delight in combining this uncommon duo

designed by **Kim Otterbein**

Metal clay components

1 Lightly oil your hands and any surfaces. Place 4–5g of metal clay between two sheet protectors and roll it out to 2 playing cards (.5mm) thick. Texture the metal clay and cut two shapes as desired.

2 Use a pin to make a hole in the middle of each metal clay shape **(photo a)**. A head pin will go through this hole to attach the metal clay to a polymer form. Dry the clay, and file the edges with a nail file. If you want the components to have be domed, let them dry on a rounded object such as a small ball, button, or lightbulb.

3 Fire the clay following the clay manufacturer's instructions. Allow the pieces to cool, and then polish them carefully with a brass brush. Add a patina using liver of sulfur, if desired.

Post earrings

1 Choose a shape for your earring. that's a little larger than the metal clay so the polymer shows. Draw the shape on an index card and use a craft knife to cut it out.

2 Condition the polymer clay. Once my clay is conditioned, I like to mix a couple of similar colors and then add translucent clay to one or two of them. Roll each color into a snake and

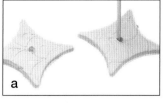

a

b

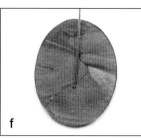

c

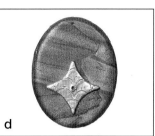

d

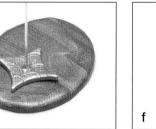

e

f

g

twist them together, folding them in half a few times **(photo b)**. Roll the clay through a pasta machine to about ¹⁄₁₆-in. (2mm) thick, and place it on a piece of parchment paper.

3 Hold the index-card template over the clay and find the areas you like best for your earrings. Place the index card on the clay and cut out your shape with a craft knife **(photo c)**. Don't cut through the parchment paper. Cut out a second piece in the same shape. Remove the excess clay, and set it aside. You'll use it later to make the backs of the earrings.

4 Put a small piece of plastic wrap over one shape. Lightly press and smooth the edges with your finger, being careful not to distort the shape. Remove the plastic wrap and smooth out any imperfections. Repeat with the other polymer shape.

5 Determine where you will position the metal clay component. Gently nudge it into place, being careful not to mar the polymer **(photo d)**. Press the metal clay component into the polymer just hard enough to make an impression. Insert a head pin through the hole in the metal clay component and

make a hole in the polymer **(photo e)**. Remove the head pin. Repeat with the other polymer shape.

6 Put the parchment and your shapes on a ceramic tile and cover them with a tent-shaped piece of foil. Bake the clay in a toaster oven following the clay manufacturer's instructions. Remove the clay, cover it with another piece of parchment, and place another tile on top. This will keep the polymer flat as it cools. If you want a highly polished piece, remove the metal clay component, and sand the polymer underwater. Start with 400-grit and progress to 600-grit or higher sandpaper.

7 With the metal clay component in place, push a head pin through the hole in the metal clay and polymer. Bend the head pin so the wire lies flat against the back of the polymer **(photo f)**. Trim the end, leaving an ¹⁄₈-in. (3mm) tail.

8 To hold a post finding in place until you put the clay backing on, glue it, flat side down, to the back of a baked polymer piece using superglue.

9 The leftover clay you set aside will now be used for the back and can be textured. Texturing makes fingerprints

less obvious, but it's not necessary. To texture the clay, spritz the texture with water and press it into the clay. Place the clay on parchment and cut two pieces that are slightly larger than the baked polymer pieces.

10 With a paintbrush, apply a thin layer of liquid polymer clay to the back of a baked polymer piece, coating the head pin and post pad. Push a piece of textured clay over the post, press it onto the baked polymer **(photo g)**, and seal it around the post with

supplies:

earrings, either style
- 4–5g silver metal clay
- polymer clay, ¼ oz. in each of 2 colors plus translucent
- liquid polymer clay
- 2 ball-end 26-gauge sterling silver head pins
- acrylic roller
- aluminum foil
- spray bottle with water
- brass brush
- 2 smooth 6-in. (15cm) ceramic tiles
- chainnose pliers
- craft knife
- superglue
- index card
- torch or kiln
- liver of sulfur (optional)
- buffing machine (optional)
- nail file
- paintbrush
- parchment paper
- pasta machine
- pin
- 2 4 x 6-in. (10 x 15cm) pieces of heavyweight plastic sheet protector

- plastic wrap
- 4 playing cards
- wet/dry sandpaper (320-, 400-, and 600-grit)
- small shape cutters* (optional)
- texture sheets
- olive oil or nonpetroleum hand salve
- toaster oven*

post earrings
- 2 earring posts with flat 6–8mm pad
- 2 ear nuts

dangle earrings
- 6 in. (15cm) 20-gauge sterling silver wire, half-hard
- 1½–9 in. (3.8–23cm) 22-gauge sterling silver wire, half-hard
- steel bench block
- ³⁄₈-in. (1cm) dowel
- hammer
- roundnose pliers
- wire cutters

*Dedicated to use with polymer clay

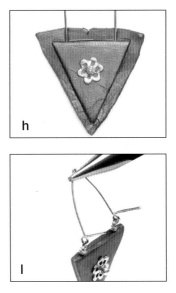

h

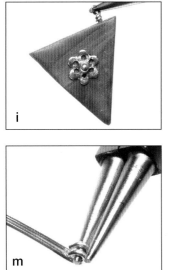

i

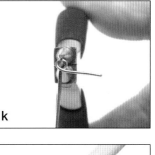

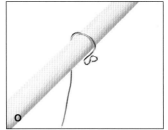

j

k

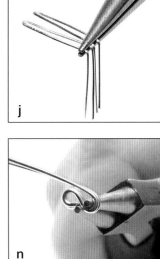

l

m

n

o

the back of your fingernail. Repeat with the other piece of textured clay and baked polymer.

11 Using your fingertips, work the air bubbles out of both pieces gently. To refine the shapes for a more delicate look, compress the edges so the pieces are slightly thinner at the sides. You will trim the excess polymer after it's baked.

12 Put the earrings face down on parchment, cover them with a foil tent, and bake them on the tile again.

13 Let the pieces cool slightly. Hold each earring face up, and being careful not to cut into the body of the earrings, trim the excess clay with a craft knife. The clay is

fragile while it's still warm, so be gentle.

14 Starting with 320-grit sandpaper, sand the edges of your earrings until you can't tell the front layer from the back. Work your way up to 600-grit and then polish the pieces on your jeans or buff them with a buffing machine.

Dangle earrings

1 Follow steps 1–7 of the post earrings.

2 Cut one or two 1½-in. (3.8cm) pieces of 22-gauge wire, depending on whether you are going to hang your earring from a single loop, as in the brown-and-turquoise earrings, or from two loops, as in the blue-and-green earrings, or if you're going to add a dangle.

3 Follow step 9 of the post earrings. Flip the backing texture side down, and position the end ⅛–¼ in. (3–6mm) of the wire(s) where you want to position the wrapped loop(s). Apply a thin layer of liquid polymer clay to the back surface of a baked polymer shape, and place it over the back piece (photo h).

4 Follow step 11 of the post earrings. Gently remove the wires, leaving a hole into

which the wires will be reinserted later. Follow steps 12–14.

5 Make a wrapped loop with a 1½-in. (3.8cm) piece of wire. Trim the stem to ⅛–¼ in. (3–6mm), and check the fit in a hole you made in step 4. The bottom of the wraps should be flush against the earring. Trim more wire if necessary. With chainnoise pliers, slightly flatten the tip of the wire, dab it with superglue, and insert it into a hole (photo i). Nothing wrecks a polymer project faster than a stray drop of superglue, so be careful! Hold the loop in place for 10 seconds. Repeat if you're using two loops.

6 If you're using a single loop, skip to step 8 to make the earring wires. For earrings with two loops, cut two 3-in. (7.6cm) pieces of 22-gauge wire. Keeping the two wires together, bend them in half. Using chainnose pliers, grasp all four wire ends ¾ in. (1.9cm) from the fold, and make a right-angle bend (photo j). With the tip of your roundnose pliers, make the first half of a wrapped loop on each end (photo k).

7 Open the folded end of one wire to the same width as the distance between the wrapped loops stuck into the polymer. Slide both loops through the loops in the polymer (photo l), and finish the wraps to make a decorative wire triangle. Repeat for the other earring.

8 Cut two 3-in. (7.6cm) pieces of 20-gauge wire. Holding them together, bend the tips of the wires with roundnose pliers to make a small curl (photo m). Make a curve in the opposite direction to create an "S" shape (photo n). One at a time, bend the long wire ends around a ⅜-in. (1cm) dowel to make the shape of an earring wire (photo o). Trim the ends. Place the earring on a steel bench block, and gently hammer the part that goes through your ear. Attach a wrapped loop or wire triangle to each earring wire.

EDITOR'S NOTE:
To make holes for the wires after baking, use a twist drill or Flex Shaft with a #72 bit.

Planet pink

Go into orbit
with this unique
combination of metal
clay, polymer clay,
and crystals

designed by **Lisa Pavelka**

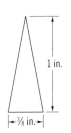

1 in.

⅜ in.

FIGURE (ACTUAL SIZE)

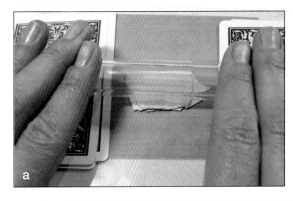

a

b

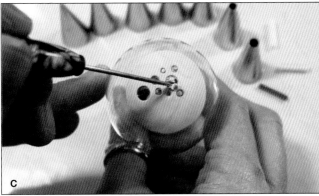

c

d

e

supplies:

pendant, 1½-in. (3.8cm) diameter

- 10g low-fire silver metal clay
- 2 oz. polymer clay in each of **3** colors: white, raspberry, plum
- **6–10** 2–4mm crystal chatons in assorted colors
- acrylic roller
- agate burnisher
- awl
- butane torch
- 1¼-in. (3.2cm) circle cutter
- coffee-stirring straw
- cosmetic sponge
- craft knife
- deli or parchment paper
- rotary tool with assorted bits (optional)
- food dehydrator*
- G-S Hypo Cement
- index card
- high-temp poly bonder glue
- iridescent foil for polymer
- needle tool
- olive oil or nonpetroleum hand salve
- pasta machine*
- plastic food wrap

- **8** playing cards
- round jeweler's file
- rubber work block
- ruler
- sandpaper (400-,800-, 2000-, 4000-grit)
- scissors
- small paintbrush
- small piece of fire blanket
- small, round vanity lightbulb
- smooth ceramic tile
- flexible Teflon sheet
- tissue blade
- toaster oven*
- tweezers
- Wilton round cake-icing tips #1–8, or assorted size drinking straws
- wire brush

*Dedicated to use with polymer clay

Working with metal clay is simple when you use an inexpensive butane torch, available at cooking stores. Then add pink pizzazz to make it pop!

Metal clay components

1 Using a cosmetic sponge, lightly oil the acrylic roller and your hands with olive oil or hand salve. Working on a flexible Teflon sheet, roll out the metal clay to 4 cards thick (**photo a**).

2 Drape the clay over the dome of a lightbulb, and gently smooth it with your palm. Using a circle cutter, cut out a dome (**photo b**). Leave the clay on the bulb. Immediately rewrap and store any leftover metal clay. (Do this after every cutting or trimming step.)

3 Using cake-icing tips or drinking straws, punch out various sized holes in the clay dome. Use an awl to remove the dots of clay (**photo c**). Be sure to leave plenty of clay between the holes and around the edges to ensure the finished piece's strength.

4 To make a tube bail, draw a triangle 1 in. (2.5cm) high by ⅜ in. (1cm) wide on an index card (**figure**). Cut out the triangle. Using leftover metal clay from steps 2 and 3, roll the clay between two 2-card (.5mm) stacks of playing cards. Place the triangle on the clay, and trim around it with a craft knife. Beginning with the wide end, roll the clay triangle around a stir straw 1½ times, leaving the narrow end flat and extended in a point. Cut a triangle ¼ in. (6mm) wide by ¾ in. (1.9cm) tall from the leftover clay. Place the new triangle around the tube bail, with the point facing in the same direction as the bail's pointed tip (**photo d**). Let the clay dome and bail dry.

5 With the dome still on the lightbulb, lightly sand the top surface of the dome, working through the sandpaper grits from coarse to fine (**photo e**). Using a paintbrush, brush away the clay dust after sanding between each grit. Repeat for the bail while still on the straw.

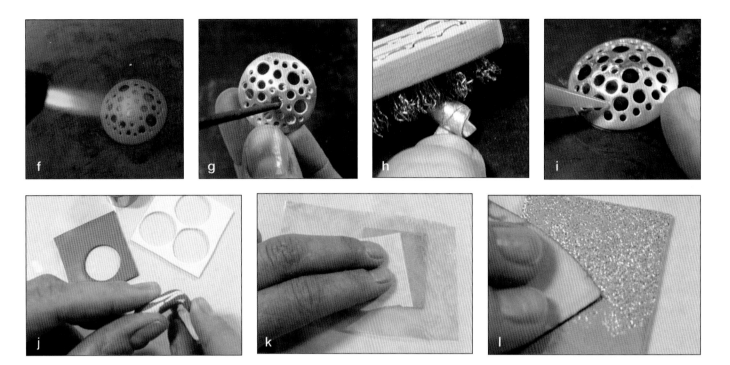

6 Carefully remove the dome from the lightbulb, and gently twist the straw to loosen it from the dried bail. Place the dome and the bail on the fire blanket. In a dimly lit, well-ventilated room, ignite the butane torch. Hold the torch 4–6 in. (10–15cm) from the bail, and continually move the torch to distribute the heat evenly. When the piece appears to be a peach color, begin timing the firing for two minutes, maintaining the peach color the entire time (photo f). If the color becomes pale, bring the torch closer until you see peach. If the piece appears shiny or the color looks red, back the torch away to prevent melting. Allow the piece to cool on its own, or pick it up with tweezers and drop it into water to quench. Repeat for the bail.

7 Using a round file or optional rotary tool, refine and clean the edges of the holes in the dome (photo g).

8 Working on a rubber block, brush both pieces firmly with a wire brush until the surface begins to appear metallic (photo h).

9 Using an agate burnisher, burnish both pieces firmly to bring out the shine (photo i).

Polymer clay components

Wash your hands every time you switch clay colors. Use a smooth ceramic tile for your work surface.

1 Condition each block of clay. Set a pasta machine to the thickest setting, and roll out 1 oz. of white clay and ⅓ oz. of raspberry clay. Using the circle cutter, cut three disks of white clay and one disk of raspberry clay. Mix the disks together (photo j) until blended to a pastel pink color.

2 Set the pasta machine to the medium setting, and roll out the blended clay, making sure it measures at least 2 x 2 in. (5 x 5cm).

Following the clay manufacturer's instructions, apply iridescent foil to the rolled-out sheet (photo k). Press very coarse sandpaper onto the foiled clay to create texture (photo l).

3 Apply poly bonder glue to the back of the pointed tip of the bail, and press the bail into the textured surface of the foiled clay along the top edge. Cut a corner off the foiled clay, and press it down

DESIGNER'S TIPS:
- Drying times for metal clay depend upon climate. To speed the drying process, you can use a food dehydrator, hot plate, or toaster oven set at 200°F (93°C).
- Dried, unfired metal clay is as delicate as a potato chip, so handle it with extreme care.
- When you start firing metal clay, you will see a flame for a few seconds. This is the clay binder burning off.
- Metal clay will shrink between 8 and 10 percent as the binder burns off.
- If in doubt about holding at the proper temperature long enough, add an extra minute of torch time. As long as the piece doesn't turn red, you cannot over-fire it.
- Any holes that appear slightly distorted are ideal for crystal settings, as the chatons will camouflage imperfections.
- After firing metal clay, the surface appears white due to silver molecules standing upright. You can burnish the piece to a typical silver appearance.
- For a more pronounced mirror finish, sand again with all four grits of sandpaper before using the agate burnisher.
- Use a silver polishing cloth or pad to periodically polish your silver.

METAL CLAY

m

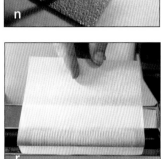

n

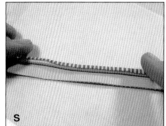

o

p

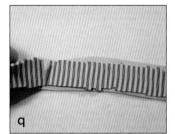

q

r

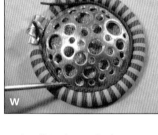

s

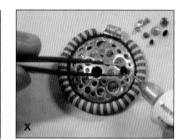

t

u

v

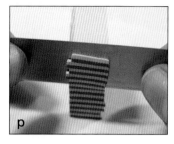

w

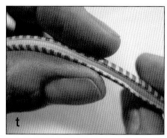

x

over the exposed tip of the bail. Texture with sandpaper to conceal the tip **(photo m)**.

4 Apply poly bonder glue to the bottom edge of the silver dome, and, aligning it with the base of the tube bail, press the dome firmly into the foiled clay. Using a craft knife, trim away the excess clay **(photo n)**. Bake, following the clay manufacturer's instructions, for 10 minutes.

5 Set the pasta machine to the medium setting, and roll a 2 x 2-in. (5 x 5cm) sheet of pastel pink clay and a 2 x 2-in. sheet of raspberry clay. Stack the sheets on top of each other, and use a tissue blade to trim the edges **(photo o)**. Roll the two layers through the pasta machine.

6 Cut the clay sheet in half, and stack one layer on top of the other with colors alternating. Repeat. Cut in thirds, and stack the pieces to form a striped stack. Using the tissue blade, cut a slice 1⁄16 in. (2mm) thick **(photo p)**. Repeat to cut three more slices.

7 Set the pasta machine to the thickest setting, and roll a strip of pastel pink clay that is 1⁄2 x 5 in. (1.3 x 13cm). Place the striped slices end-to-end on the pink strip **(photo q)**. Lightly smooth the slices together by rolling them widthwise with an acrylic roller.

8 Set the pasta machine to the thick setting. Place a piece of deli or parchment paper over the striped sheet, and roll it through the pasta machine with the stripes aligned vertically against the rollers **(photo r)**.

9 Roll a snake of pastel pink clay that is 1⁄16 x 4 1⁄2 in. (2mm x 11.4cm). Trim one edge of the striped sheet, and wrap it around the snake **(photo s)**. Trim the striped sheet to leave a small gap along the length of the roll **(photo t)**.

10 Cut one end of the striped roll straight, and use poly bonder to glue the roll, with the gap facing inward, around the outer edge of the baked and cooled dome **(photo u)**. Using the craft knife, trim the ends that meet the bail at a 45-degree angle **(photo v)**.

11 Roll out a very thin snake of plum clay, about 1⁄32 in. (1mm) diameter and 4 1⁄2 in. (11.4cm) long. Nest this snake around the inner edge of the striped clay. Decorate and secure it by using a needle tool to mark diagonal lines in line with each stripe **(photo w)**. Trim and remove excess clay. Bake for 30 minutes.

12 This step is optional for finishing the back: Make a sheet of foiled pink clay, following the process in step 2. Cut a disk with the circle cutter. Use poly bonder to glue the disk to the back of the pendant, foiled side out, and bake again for 15 minutes.

13 Using G-S Hypo Cement and tweezers, glue crystal chatons into several of the dome holes **(photo x)**. Allow to set overnight before threading the bail onto a neck cord or chain to wear.

Clay in clay

Make a metal clay frame to showcase a polymer clay image transfer

designed by **Debbie Carlton**

supplies:

pendant, 3 x 1-in. (7.6 x 2.5cm)

- 15–20g silver metal clay
- metal clay slip
- polymer clay
  - 2 oz. pearl
  - 1 oz. scrap
- photocopies: black-and-white or color, toner based (not ink-jet)
- cardstock
- craft knife
- playing cards
- flexible Teflon sheet
- olive oil or natural hand balm
- texture sheet (optional)
- shaping tool
- carving tools (optional)
- cup bur (optional)
- fine-grit sanding pad
- fine-tip paintbrush
- drinking straw
- needle files
- kiln
- finishing items (choose from): brass brush, tumbler with steel shot and burnishing compound, liver of sulfur
- acrylic roller or pasta machine*
- bone folder
- spray bottle with water
- toaster oven*
- needle tool
- latex gloves

*Dedicated to use with polymer clay

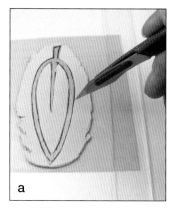

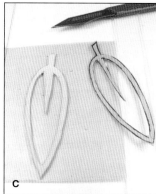

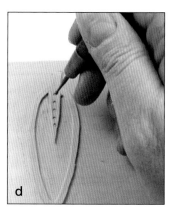

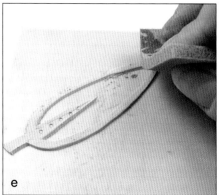

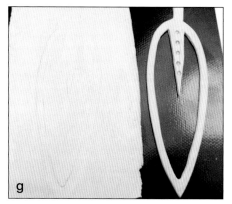

Incorporate polymer clay and metal clay to make a pendant. You'll use a template to make a metal clay frame assembly. That frame, once fired, is used to make a polymer clay template for a polymer clay inlay. You'll use a direct image-transfer technique to apply a black-and-white photocopy to light-colored polymer clay prior to inserting the inlay into the metal clay frame. You can introduce color by using polymer clay in vibrant hues. Or, make your insert from a sheet of textured or patterned polymer clay.

Metal clay frame

1 Draw your desired pendant frame onto a sheet of cardstock. See "Sources of Inspiration," p. 93, for ideas for template shapes. Use a craft knife to cut out the frame template.
2 On a flexible Teflon sheet, roll 10g of metal clay to 4 playing cards (1mm) thick. Place the frame template on the sheet of clay. Using a craft knife, carefully cut along the outside line **(photo a)** of the frame template and along the inside line **(photo b)**. Remove the excess clay. When the metal clay is semi-dry (still moist, but holds its shape), remove the template **(photo c)**.

3 Add texture either with an oiled texture sheet or by using a shaping tool, or let the clay frame dry completely and then carve designs into it using carving tools. I used a small cup bur to carve circles into the surface of my dry frame **(photo d)**.
4 When the frame is completely dry, use a fine-grit sanding pad to refine the frame's surface and edges **(photo e)**.
5 Make the back panel: Roll 8g of metal clay to 3 cards (.75mm) thick. Lay the metal clay frame face up on the sheet of clay **(photo f)**. Gently press the frame into the sheet to leave the frame's indentation. Carefully remove the frame **(photo g)**. Use a craft knife to cut out the back panel by cutting on the median line between the frame's inner and outer edges **(photo h)**.
6 Place the frame face down on your work surface. Use a fine-tip paintbrush to apply metal clay slip to the back of the frame and to the outer edges of the front of the back panel.
7 Position the back panel on the frame so that the back panel covers the frame's opening. Use a smoothing tool to gently tack the back panel to the frame. I used my cup bur **(photo i)**. Set the frame assembly aside until it's semi-dry.

8 Turn the frame assembly face-up and use the fine-tip paintbrush to apply metal clay slip to the join **(photo j)**. Allow the frame assembly to dry completely, and then refine it with a fine-grit sanding pad.
9 Roll 1g of metal clay to 3 cards thick. Use a craft knife to cut the clay into a 1 x ⅛-in. (2.5cm x 3mm) strip. Add texture as desired **(photo k)**.
10 Use the fine-tip paintbrush to apply metal clay slip to one end of the strip. Attach that part of the strip to the back of the assembly. (For added stability, I attached my strip to the back of the stem, at the top of my assembly). Use a drinking straw to support the strip as you shape it into a bail. Use slip to attach the remaining end of the strip to the assembly's back **(photo l)**. Set the assembly aside until it's completely dry.
11 Remove the straw, and refine the bail and back of the assembly with the fine-grit sanding pad and needle files.
12 Fire the assembly according to the metal clay manufacturer's instructions. Polish the assembly with a brass brush and soapy water, or tumble-polish it in a tumbler with steel shot and burnishing compound **(photo m)**. If desired, apply a

Contributors

Tea Benduhn is an associate editor at *Bead&Button* magazine. Contact her at tbenduhn@beadandbutton.com.

Jana Roberts Benzon is a full-time artist, creating wearable art from her studio in Salt Lake City. Contact her at jana@janarobertsbenzon.com, or via her website, janarobertsbenzon.com.

Debbie Carlton is a designer-maker specializing in contemporary jewelry combining polymer and metal clay. She lives and teaches both materials from her workshop in London. Contact her via her website, debbiecarltonjewellery.co.uk, her blog, http://polymerand metalclayheaven.blogspot.com, or at info@debbiecarltonjewellery.co.uk.

Nancy Clark has been a bead artist for 10 years. She says the possibilities in beading and polymer clay are endless and enjoys experimenting with new techniques. Contact her by email at rocketdogbeads@comcast.net

Jeffrey Lloyd Dever received his Bachelors of Fine Arts degree from Atlantic Union College in 1976 and has been in the field of graphic design and illustration ever since. He is founding partner of the award-winning studio Dever Designs (1985) and its subsidiary Fresh Art, located in Laurel, Maryland. He is on the adjunct faculty for illustration and graphic design at the Maryland Institute College of Art in Baltimore, Md. and as a teacher/consultant at Southern Adventist University in Collegedale, Tenn. Jeff's 3-D illustrations have received numerous awards and his vessels have been represented in several national survey exhibitions.

Contact **Barbara Fajardo** at rubarb04@hotmail.com, or visit her website, rubarbdesertdesigns.com, to see more of her work.

Christi Friesen is an award-winning artist and author of polymer clay books and projects. Contact her and view more of her work online at CForiginals.com.

An award-winning polymer and metal clay artist and designer, **Patricia Kimle** has contributed more than 30 project articles to magazines and has written a book about combining polymer and metal clay entitled *Perfectly Paired*. She is a member of the International Polymer Clay Association and is a designer member of the Craft and Hobby Association. Contact Patricia via e-mail at patti@kimledesigns.com.

Visit **Desiree McCrorey's** website, desirecreations.com, to see more of her work.

Barbara McGuire has written more than 10 books on art instruction and developed templates, stamps, and molds for jewelry clays. She appeared more than 25 times on the Carol Duvall show and currently is the founder and education director at WOMAN Creative Art and Jewelry Design Center. Contact her at barbara@barbara mcguire.com or visit her website, barbaramcguire.com.

Dotty McMillan likes to turn ordinary objects into extraordinary items. Her work appears in numerous galleries, magazines, and books. In addition to her polymer clay art, she writes novels under the name Dorothy McMillan. Contact her via e-mail at dmcmillan01@earthlink.net.

Cassy Muronaka has been working with polymer clay for more than 15 years. She writes a blog, "Sometimes Daily, Always Random" at cassymuronaka.wordpress.com, and can be reached at cassymuronaka@yahoo.com.

Kim Otterbein teaches bead, clay and metals classes at The Bead House in Bristol, R.I. To see her work, visit her website, thebeadhouse.com.

Lisa Pavelka is an award-winning artist and author, as well as a frequent television guest and magazine contributor, renown for her expertise in several mediums and her signature product line. Visit her website, www.lisapavelka.com.

Contact **Melanie West** in care of Kalmbach Books.

Lori Wilkes is an artist, teacher, and author of many project articles, along with the polymer clay installment of *The Absolute Beginners Guide* series, Kalmbach Books, 2012. To see more of her work, visit millori.com. Lori welcomes email at millori.art@gmail.com.

Pam Wynn began making polymer clay beads in the early '90s when she couldn't find an adequate variety of beads in her local art-supply store. Contact her at wynnfour@mchsi.com, or visit the website she shares with her daughter Heather, heatherwynn.com.

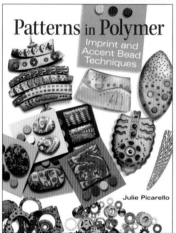
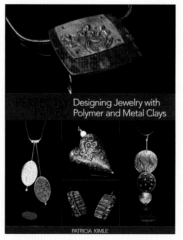

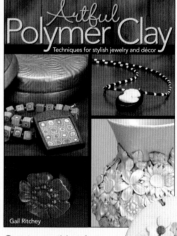

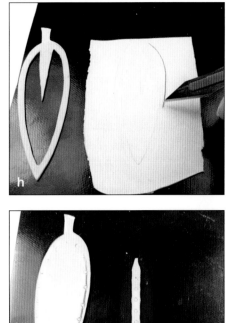

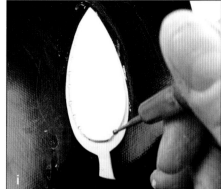

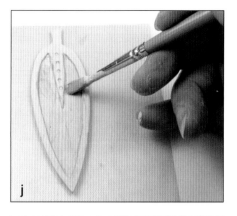

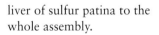

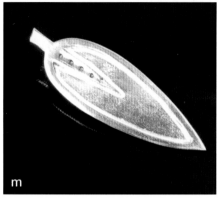

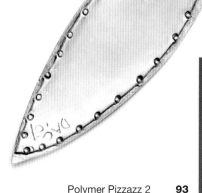

liver of sulfur patina to the whole assembly.

Polymer clay insert

1 The technique that you'll use to transfer images to polymer clay is an easy and direct method that requires you to use toner-based prints of either black-and-white or color images. Images made on ink-jet printers and copiers will not work for this transfer process.

2 Select copyright-free images or your own drawings or photographs to copy. If necessary, use the "mirror" setting on the copy machine so the image will be correctly oriented after you transfer it. To economize, use the "multiple image" setting of the copy machine to make several images on a single sheet of copy paper. See "Color Options," p. 94, for tips on adding color to a black-and-white image transfer.

3 Transfer an image onto polymer clay: Condition 1 oz. of pearl clay. Run the clay through a pasta machine set to a medium-thin setting, or use an acrylic roller to roll the clay into a sheet.

4 Place the photocopy image side down onto the clay sheet. Use a bone folder to burnish the back of the paper to ensure that the entire image is in contact with the clay **(photo n)**.

5 Spray the paper with water to fully saturate it **(photo o)**. Beginning at the center of the paper, use the pad of your fingertip to make small, circular motions to rub off the paper **(photo p)**. Rewet the paper as necessary, and

Use a cup bur to make a pattern on the bail and to press the front and back panels together.

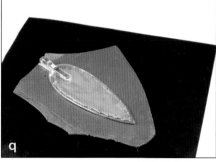

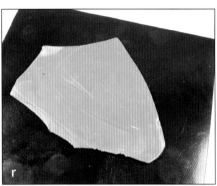

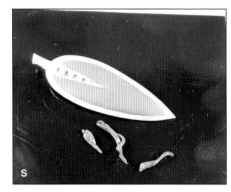

continue to rub off any remaining paper. The image will transfer to the surface of the clay.

6 Make a polymer clay template for the insert. Condition 1 oz. of scrap polymer clay, and run it through the pasta machine set to a medium-thin setting.

7 Press the metal clay assembly face down onto the polymer clay sheet **(photo q)** to make an impression of the frame. Remove the metal clay assembly **(photo r)**. Use a craft knife to cut out the polymer clay template.

8 Fit the template into the front of the metal clay frame, and trim any excess polymer clay **(photo s)**. Bake the metal clay assembly and template according to the polymer clay manufacturer's instructions. Allow the assembly to cool, and then use a needle tool to pry out the baked polymer clay template.

9 Trace the polymer clay template onto a piece of cardstock. Use a craft knife to cut out the shape of the template, so you create a window template.

10 Select an area of the image transfer for the image insert. Use the cardstock window template to select the portion of the polymer clay image transfer that you want to insert into the metal clay frame. Once you've selected the composition, use a needle tool to lightly score a line along the interior edge of the window template.

11 Cut out the image insert. Place the polymer clay template within the scored outline on the image transfer. Use the craft knife to cut around the polymer clay template to create the image insert for the frame **(photos t and u)**.

12 Embed the insert into the frame. Wear latex gloves and place the image insert into the metal clay frame. Gently press the edges of the image insert so that it completely fills the frame **(photo v)**.

13 Bake the pendant according to the polymer clay manufacturer's instructions.

COLOR OPTIONS:
Try any of the following methods to introduce color into your pendant design:
- **Mix a little bit of colored clay into the pearl clay before you transfer your image.**
- **Make a polymer clay insert from a Skinner blend.**
- **Use alcohol-based inks to paint on the transferred image before you cure the pendant.**
- **Brush on some iridescent powders or paint after the pendant is cured. Seal the image with a coat of clear polymer clay glaze.**